New Dawn
The GODDESS AWAKENS

TINA PENNYCUICK

Copyright © 2025 Tina Pennycuick

All rights reserved. No part of this publication may be reproduced, stored in a retrieval system, or transmitted in any form or by any means — electronic, mechanical, photocopying, recording, or otherwise — without the prior written permission of the author, except in the case of brief quotations for review, comment, or academic purposes.

First published in Great Britain in 2025

by Tina Pennycuick

ISBN: 978-1-0684440-0-5

This is a work of memoir and personal reflection. Some names, places, and identifying details have been changed to protect the privacy of individuals.

Cover design by Izabela Novoselec

Interior design by Izabela Novoselec

British Library Cataloguing-in-Publication Data

A catalogue record for this book is available from the British Library.

Printed and bound in the United Kingdom

For permissions, media, or speaking inquiries:

tinalpennycuick@gmail.com

PREFACE:

A Journey to Balance and Awakening

Reflecting on my life, I see a tapestry woven with triumphs and tribulations. For years, I chased success, only to find myself lost in the life I had built. From the outside, it seemed I had everything figured out: a successful career, a beautiful home, financial stability—everything I was taught to strive for.

Yet, beneath the surface, something was missing.

No promotion, salary increase, or external success could fill the void growing inside me. I had become lost in the life I had built, playing the expected role yet disconnected from my truth. The stress, relentless pressure, and slow unravelling of my personal life left me feeling hollow. I had spent years proving myself to the world, but what if I had never known myself?

In my darkest moments, when everything around me felt like it was falling apart, I began searching—not just for relief, but for something more profound.

At first, healing came in small, tangible ways—crystals, Reiki, and energy work. I turned to these practices out of desperation, seeking peace amidst the chaos. But what started as survival slowly became transformation.

Each step deeper into this world peeled back another layer of myself. Through yoga retreats, sound baths, and the guidance of extraordinary women, I started remembering parts of myself I had long buried—the intuitive, the seeker, the woman who had a voice beyond the boardroom.

And then came the fundamental shift—the Goddess retreat in Zanzibar.

It was here, surrounded by women's power, the wisdom of ancient rituals, and the ocean's unshakable presence, that the Goddess within me awakened.

I learned that the challenges I faced—especially in the corporate world—were not just obstacles to overcome. They were mirrors, reflecting the lessons I needed to learn.

I had spent my life shrinking, silencing myself, making space for others at the cost of my truth. But through the ceremony and deep inner work, I began reclaiming my voice.

And perhaps the most profound lesson of all?

Love starts with you.

For years, I searched for connections in relationships and achievements, even in endless swipes on dating apps, trying to find something real among the noise. But after the retreat, I stopped looking outside of myself. I finally understood that I had to embody it before I could seek love. Before I could be seen, I had to see myself.

This book, New Dawn: The Goddess Awakens, is not just about finding balance between the fast-paced world of work and the quiet call of the soul—it is about coming home to yourself.

It is about stepping into your power, truth, and voice.

It is about recognizing that the challenges, the triggers, and the people who unsettle you — are the most outstanding teachers.

It is about realizing that healing is not a destination but a practice.

For those who feel the weight of life's demands pressing down or long to break free from the roles they have been told to play, I invite you to walk this path with me.

New Dawn: The Goddess Awakens is not just my story. It is a guide, a reflection, an offering — an invitation for you to reclaim your truth, to stand fully in who you are, and to embrace the possibility of your new dawn.

.

TABLE OF CONTENTS

1. The Shadows and the Light – A Child's Journey	9
2. The Shadows of Adulthood – Relationships, Career, and Losing Myself	17
3. The Healing Power of Energy	29
4. Healing and Sisterhood - The Strength to Say No	41
5. Losing Myself in Love	53
6. Losing Myself in Work – The Distraction of Busyness	69
7. The Universe Will Always Test You	75
8. Reawakening the Goddess – A Journey Back to Myself	87
9. From Rituals to Reality	103
10. Sacred Medicine - A Deeper Awakening	113
11. Living the Goddess Within	125
12. Integration - The True Work of Living the Goddess Within	133
Acknowledgements	142

CHAPTER 1:

The Shadows and the Light

– A Child's Journey

Life as a child was a story of two halves: the light that I hold dear and the shadows that linger in the background of my memory. It is strange how time can obscure certain moments, how it buries parts of our past so profoundly that we can only catch glimpses of them when the mind wanders, or an old feeling resurfaces. My childhood was the same — a blend of joy, imagination, and innocence interwoven with darkness, pain, and confusion.

The shadows loomed large for years, and it took much of my adult life to begin shining light into those corners. Yet, even amid the chaos, there was always light, primarily through my mother. She was the brightness I clung to, her creativity and love a balm against the storms we faced.

Despite having little material wealth, she gave me the world through her compassion and imagination. We created magical worlds with what little she had, building fairy houses from long grass and making cups and tables from sticks and acorn shells. It felt like an escape but was so much more than that.

We would walk miles through nature, lost in a world of make-believe. I remember imagining fairy doors hidden in the trunks of grand oak trees, the bluebells ringing softly as dusk fell, and the feeling that we had stepped into a realm of magic. At the time, I believed it was all fantasy—a shield against the noise, the violence, and the uncertainty brewing at home. My father's temper, often fuelled by alcohol, erupted like a storm, leaving us to live on eggshells, waiting for the next outburst. In those moments when the shadows were darkest, my mother's ability to create beauty from nothing felt like salvation.

Looking back, I realise our long walks weren't just a pastime but a necessity. They were free, and they took us out of the house. I remember crouching low in a meadow near our home, my mother's hands deftly weaving blades of grass into a tiny chair for our fairy queen. "They'll visit tonight," she whispered, her eyes alight with mischief and belief. I watched her fingers, mesmerized, forgetting for a moment the noise and chaos waiting for us back home. The air smelled of wildflowers and fresh earth, and in that fleeting moment, the world felt safe magical.

I didn't understand then that these moments weren't just an escape but an introduction to a more profound truth. The connection I felt to nature, the magic of the trees, and the whispers of the wind was the beginning of a spiritual path I would one day walk with open eyes. Those fairy kingdoms we imagined weren't entirely make-believe. As an adult, I've come to understand that the magic I believed in so fervently as a little girl was my first connection to the elemental world, to the devas and the energies of the Earth. These memories, once buried, have surfaced with new clarity as I've journeyed through life, learning about healing energies, crystals, and dimensions beyond the physical.

At the time, however, it was simply survival. I was a sensitive child—watchful, wary, and deeply attuned to the energies around me. I trusted little and did everything in my power to blend into the background, to stay hidden from the chaos that felt like a permanent fixture in my home. I vividly remember hiding behind my first teacher's skirt, desperately hoping to remain invisible, praying no one would see me. That desire to be unseen followed me for much of my young life, especially at school.

The school was no sanctuary. I was caught between wanting to hide and needing to excel so I wouldn't get into trouble. I carried the world's weight on my small shoulders, feeling like I had to be perfect to avoid conflict or shame. But no matter how hard I tried, I never quite fit in. When I was eight, my mother finally gathered the courage to make a brave and necessary decision. Tired of the lies, the fights, and the violence, she moved us to another town, miles away from what we had once called home. It felt like a new beginning—a chance to break the cycle.

However, the shadows followed us. Despite my mother's best efforts, my father came back into our lives, charming his way back into her trust and dragging the old patterns with him. The cycles of drama and tension began again in this new place, and I found myself once more in a world of confusion and instability.

Fridays and Saturdays were the worst. The drink became my father's closest ally; his temper was chaotic and unpredictable. I can still remember one evening when he returned home from drinking, the crash of a bottle shattering the silence as I dove under the kitchen table, knees to my chest, heart pounding. My mother's calm voice floated through the storm, steady and soothing: "Please, not tonight." Her words were soft, but they carried the weight of someone who had weathered far too many storms. The fairy world we had built just hours before felt so far away.

As I grew older, I began to see my father's temper in the context of his world—a world where men were taught to be providers, to bury their feelings, and to hide weakness at all costs. Anger became his only language, and alcohol was his only escape. Though it doesn't excuse the damage he caused, it helps me understand the man behind the rage. My mother bore the brunt of his storms, standing as a fragile shield between his fury and us.

The tension at home followed me to school, manifesting in different ways. While I couldn't escape my father's temper, I hoped school might offer some reprieve. Instead, it became another place where I felt small and unseen. Friendships had already been formed and alliances made, and I found myself struggling to fit into a world that seemed to have no place for me. I sat on the sidelines, never truly fitting in. Bullying became a constant, and with each passing day, my confidence faded.

One memory stands out vividly: sitting in class, trying to focus on the teacher's words when the sharp sting of ink flicked onto my neck and jolted me back to reality. Laughter erupted from the back row as another drop splattered onto my notebook, ruining the notes I had painstakingly written. I clenched my jaw and stared straight ahead, refusing to give them the satisfaction of seeing my tears. Lunchtime was no refuge either—my lunch often disappeared before I could touch it, stolen by the same classmates who delighted in making me their target. "Loser," "weirdo," "ugly"—their words etched themselves into my sense of self, scars I carried silently for years.

I remember the constant battle to navigate the school day unnoticed. I learned to keep my head down, my voice quiet, and my movements small. My survival instinct was to blend in, but no matter how much I tried to disappear, the bullies always seemed to find me. The teasing chipped away at my confidence, leaving me desperate to prove my worth in other ways. I began to equate perfection with safety, believing that if I excelled, I could shield myself from ridicule. This pattern would follow me into adulthood, shaping how I approached relationships, work, and even my sense of self-worth.

By high school, things improved slightly, but the shadows of isolation remained. Even when I found a place among the "in the crowd," I still felt like an outsider, my presence tolerated rather than embraced. I spent much of my teens trying to fit in—changing my mannerisms, looks, and even my voice to match those around me. Yet, no matter how hard I tried, I stood apart, and the bullying continued, leaving lasting imprints on my confidence.

During these years, I became skilled at adapting myself to suit others. I learned how to read a room and change my tone, posture, and demeanour to fit in. It was a skill born of necessity, but it later left me questioning my true identity. Who was I beneath the masks I wore so carefully?

Through it all, my mother remained my anchor. She found ways to lift me up even when her struggles threatened to overwhelm her. I often wondered how she carried so much without breaking. There were nights when I caught her staring out the window, her face etched with exhaustion, though she'd always turn to me with a smile when she noticed me watching.

Her resilience wasn't just in surviving but in her ability to create moments of beauty despite the chaos. Whether it was crafting fairy furniture in the meadow or telling me stories about brave, magical heroines, she taught me to believe in something more significant than the darkness around us. Looking back, I realise she planted hope and strength in me, even when she couldn't see it herself.

Nature became my solace during those turbulent years. I would escape to the woods or meadows, losing myself in the earth's rhythm. The wind in the trees, the soft rustle of leaves, the sun's warmth on my skin — it all felt like a gentle reminder that there was still beauty in the world.

I didn't know it then, but these moments laid the foundation for my spiritual journey. The magic I felt in the natural world wasn't just a child's imagination — it was a connection to something sacred, something I would later explore through crystals, energy work, and meditation. Nature taught me to find peace, even in the smallest moments, and that lesson would stay with me long after I left my childhood home.

As I moved into adulthood, the patterns of my childhood began to play out in new ways. The desire to be unseen, to adapt, to avoid conflict at all costs — these instincts shaped my relationships, my career, and my sense of self. It took years to understand how deeply those early experiences had imprinted on me. The shadows of my past lingered, but so did the light.

Looking back now, I see that those early years set the stage for the rest of my life. The pain, the bullying, the fear — they all taught me resilience, even when I didn't realise it. The fairy tales and make-believe worlds my mother and I created weren't just escapes; they were lifelines. They taught me how to find light in the darkest corners, a skill essential in my later journey of healing and growth.

As a woman in my fifties, I now know that those fairy tales, the make-believe worlds of my childhood, were my first step into a spiritual understanding of life. The faeries, the elementals, and the energies of nature were not just figments of my imagination. They were honest and guided me, even then, toward the spiritual path I would later walk. My connection to nature, magic, and the unseen forces of the world was a gift I have carried with me throughout my life.

Childhood, for me, was a tapestry woven with threads of light and shadow. It was a time of wonder and pain, of hope and fear. But above all, it was a time of learning—lessons that would shape the woman I would become. The light my mother instilled in me, the strength I found in nature, and the resilience I built in the face of adversity prepared me for something greater. They prepared me for a journey I would only begin to understand much later in life—a journey toward balance, healing, and awakening.

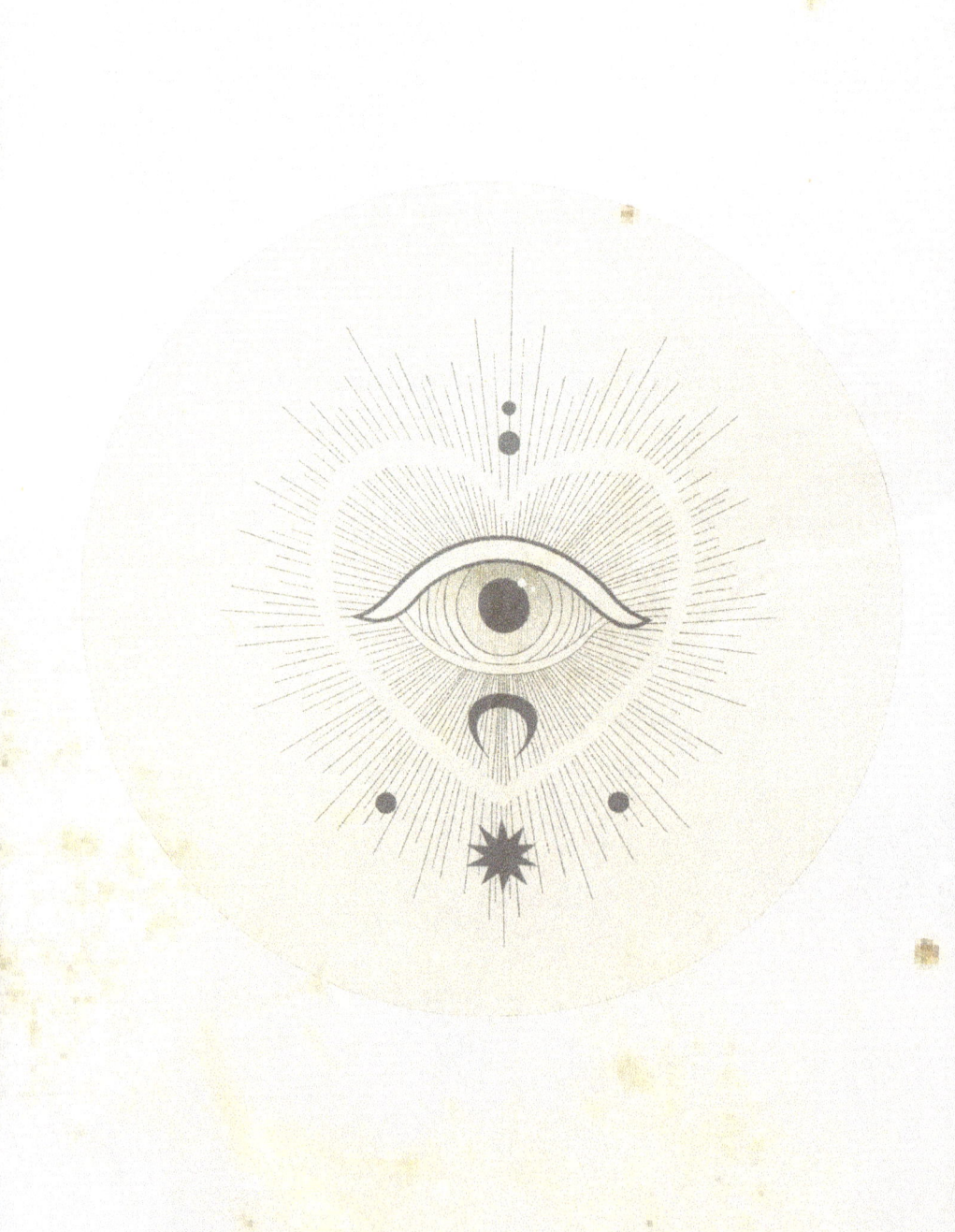

CHAPTER 2:

The Shadows of Adulthood – Relationships, Career, and Losing Myself

Throughout my teens and adulthood, my childhood's shadows continued to linger. The patterns I had learned—blending into the background, avoiding conflict, and striving for perfection—shaped every decision I made. They seeped into my relationships, career, and sense of self, creating a cycle I was too close to recognise.

When I was 18, my mother finally found the courage to divorce my father. It should have been a moment of freedom for both of us—a chance to breathe without his anger looming over our lives. Instead, his attention turned toward me, a new target for the storms he could no longer unleash on her.

One memory stands out sharply: I had just finished a shift at the technology firm where I worked. Snow fell softly as I parked in the driveway, relieved to be home. Moments later, my father's car pulled in, his headlights cutting through the dark. His face was already twisted with rage as he got out. "Why the hell are you in my spot?" he roared, his voice echoing through the stillness. Before I could respond, he moved toward me, his fist raised.

At that moment, something shifted inside me. I knew I couldn't stay. My mother and I had been sharing a room while the divorce dragged on, but I couldn't endure another day in that house. I begged my boyfriend to let me move in with him that night. It wasn't about love—it was about survival. Soon, we bought our first home together. It was small and modest, but it was mine. It was the first step toward a life that felt like my own.

My mother had spent her life working in factories, enduring grueling hours and low pay to keep food on the table. She accepted it as her lot in life, coming from a large family with few opportunities. But I wanted more. I tried to escape the cycle of struggle and scarcity that had defined her world—and mine.

In school, I dreamed of becoming an architect. I loved the idea of designing functional and beautiful structures that would stand the test of time. When I shared this dream with my headmaster, I hoped for encouragement. Instead, his words crushed me: "You're not bright enough. You'll never make it to university."

His dismissal stung, but it also lit a fire in me. I'll prove him wrong, I thought. I'll find a way. I began writing to every company on the local factory estate, pleading for a chance to work and prove myself. Eventually, I landed a job and threw myself into it with everything I had. Within 18 months, I had earned two promotions. The taste of success was intoxicating, but it came with a price.

My relentless drive to succeed began to strain my relationships. My boyfriend, who had once been my haven, started to feel like a stranger. As I climbed the corporate ladder, the dynamic between us shifted. My achievements seemed to intimidate him, widening the gulf between us.

The harder I pushed forward, the more I felt him pulling away.

At work, I faced challenges I hadn't anticipated. My ambition and enthusiasm, qualities I had always prided myself on, were often misunderstood. Some saw me as a threat; others saw me as an opportunity.

Despite these challenges, I continued to climb. I moved between industries, gained new skills, and achieved tremendous success. But my relationships followed a troubling pattern. Partners cheated on me, or I outgrew them. Each breakup left behind shards of what had once felt like love, pieces I didn't know how to put back together.

My first real opportunity to be my own boss came in the print industry. I co-founded a business with a husband-and-wife team that we hoped to grow and sell for a fortune. During this time, I met the man who would become the father of my children. He was everything I thought I wanted: charming, driven, and full of promises. He swept me off my feet, opening my eyes to a world of material luxury—fine dining, designer clothes, sparkling jewelry. I fell deeply in love, and soon after, I became pregnant with our first child.

For a while, it felt like a fairy tale. But after the birth of our son, cracks began to show. Late nights, hidden texts, and excuses that didn't quite add up—I couldn't silence the whispers of intuition. The moment I discovered the truth remains as vivid as the day it happened.

I had taken my baby, just a week old, into his workplace to show him off. His beauty and charm enchanted the women there, gathering around us with coos and smiles. All except one. She stayed at her desk, avoiding eye contact. My stomach sank, my instincts locking onto her.

I didn't want to believe it, but deep down, I knew.

From there, the breadcrumbs led me to more undeniable signs. One day, while he was out, I searched his pockets and found a receipt—for a diamond ring—a ring I didn't own. My heart raced as I unlocked his phone using a PIN so predictable it made me angry. I didn't know what I expected to find, but the voice message I uncovered made me sick. A woman's voice, soft and familiar, said how much she missed him and couldn't wait to see him again.

My world shattered. My newborn baby lay peacefully upstairs, unaware that everything we'd built was crumbling around us. I felt a wave of nausea and despair so intense I could barely stand. What was I supposed to do? I became distraught, desperate for someone to talk to. I called the young girl who helped me care for my son, and through tears, I shared the truth of what I had discovered.

Then the phone rang. It was him. I don't know how he knew, but he sounded sharp and suspicious. I bluffed through the conversation, but I made a fatal mistake in shock and panic. I didn't hang up the phone properly after the call. He heard everything—the tearful conversation, my broken voice confessing the betrayal.

That night is burned into my memory. He came home, his face twisted with anger and his voice seething as he confronted me about what he had overheard. The violence came swiftly—he pinned me against the wall, his hands gripping me so tightly that I could barely breathe. The terror in his eyes, the fury in his voice—it was like a nightmare I couldn't wake up from.

Then came the final blow. He threw me out of the house, our baby in my arms and a single plastic bin liner holding what little I could grab. The cold night air stung my face as I carried my son to the car, his tiny body warm against mine. His headlights loomed in my rearview mirror, each erratic swerve sending waves of terror through me. When I reached my mother's house, I was shaking so badly I could barely unbuckle my son.

I stayed in my mother's tiny box room for a time, a space that offered safety but little else. My son slept in a travel cot by my side, and while the room was cramped, it felt like a refuge—a space where I could begin to breathe again. My mother, ever the quiet pillar of strength, did her best to support me, though I could see the worry etched on her face. There were nights when I would catch her glancing toward my son and me, her eyes heavy with unspoken questions: How did it come to this? But she never asked, never pried. She let me be.

During those first weeks, I was in survival mode. My days were spent trying to maintain some semblance of normalcy—looking after my baby, searching for a new home, and working through the logistics of rebuilding my life. But at night, when the world grew quiet, the weight of everything I'd endured would crash over me. I would cry silently, not wanting to wake my son, as the memories of that night replayed in my mind like a relentless storm.

Eventually, I managed to buy a home of my own. It was a modest house, but it was mine—a sanctuary where I finally hoped to find stability and peace for my son and me. I poured myself into creating a warm, inviting space, painting the walls with soft colors and filling the rooms with light. On the outside, it seemed like I was piecing my life back together. But inside, I was still broken.

Despite everything, I allowed him back into our lives. He charmed his way back in with promises of change, vows of commitment, and declarations of love. Part of me wanted to believe him—to think that the man I had fallen in love with could still be the father my son deserved. But another part of me, shaped by years of shadows, feared raising a child alone. I thought I was doing the right thing, but deep down, I knew better.

Predictably, the cycle repeated itself. The lies, the gaslighting, and the manipulation were all there, just beneath the surface. The truth again revealed itself when I became pregnant with our second child. He had been unfaithful. This time, I found the strength to end it for good. I threw him out, vowing never to let him back into my life.

Being a single mother to two young children was a challenge I wasn't prepared for. My youngest became ill shortly after he was born, his tiny body struggling against relentless respiratory issues. I spent sleepless nights by his side, listening to his labored breathing, my heart breaking with every strained inhale. One night, his condition worsened, and I rushed him to the hospital. Desperate for support, I dialled my ex, hoping against hope that he might step up. But he was in Monaco with his new girlfriend, unreachable and uninterested.

I hung up the phone, tears streaming down my face, and realized the harsh truth: I was utterly alone. The weight of it all—work, motherhood, and sheer exhaustion—had pushed me to a breaking point. I became two people: the woman who got up every morning, fed and dressed her children, and went to work, and the woman who collapsed each night, too broken to face the world. Home became my sanctuary—not because it offered peace, but because it allowed me to hide. I avoided phone calls, ignored invites, and shut myself off from everyone except my boys.

During this time, I knew something had to change. I reached out to a counsellor, desperate for relief, though the thought of opening up to a stranger terrified me. My first session felt awkward—my words stumbled out with hesitation and tears. But my counsellor, a kind woman with warm eyes and a calm demeanour, didn't rush me. She listened, gently guiding me through the tangled web of emotions I had buried for so long.

I gradually found my feet again and resumed climbing the corporate ladder. I had a successful job and a beautiful home I had lovingly created for me and the boys, and I was determined not to let old wounds prevent me from finding happiness. I felt in control of my life for the first time in a long time. I met a man at work, and for a time, I enjoyed flirting, dating, and rediscovering the joys of simply living.

But life has a way of twisting in ways you can't predict. He was involved in a car accident that left him with a broken back and a broken foot. In his time of need, I invited him into my home so I could help care for him. What began as an act of compassion slowly evolved into something else. To this day, I'm not entirely sure how we ended up planning a wedding. His words still haunt me: Life is for living in the present, not dwelling in the past. He urged me to embrace the future we could create together, and I convinced myself that perhaps he was right.

Again, I ignored the signs. Despite knowing with all my heart on the wedding day that this was not meant to be, I convinced myself to go through with it. These constant moments of ignoring my truth—of silencing what my body so desperately tried to tell me—would later come to haunt me in my fifties. Yet again, the universe guided me down a path I wasn't ready for.

Shortly after getting married, and at his insistence, he left. One day, he was there; the next, he couldn't cope with married life or its responsibilities. He wanted out. He left.

By then, I had an established business and had once again found success. Yet, as before, it all started to unravel. I fell for the charms of my boss, for whom I was freelancing. I'm not proud to admit that we began an affair. I fell hard, sincerely desiring to be loved in the way I knew I could love. But he, too, was a liar and a cheat, and it ended badly.

The next relationship followed the same pattern. At that point, standing at the crossroads of my repetitive heartbreak, the second pivotal moment of change in my life occurred. I found myself in a relationship with someone who embodied light and shadow. He was fun yet deeply depressed, charming yet completely devastating. I felt responsible for him, convinced it was my role to fix him, to mend what was broken.

While searching for help, I contacted a counsellor, hoping she could guide me on how to save him. Saving people would later become a pattern I'd learn to understand—and break—but it felt like my mission at the time. I'll never forget her response. As I poured out my concerns for him, she listened quietly. Then, with calm assurance, she said, "Let's start with you, shall we?"

That moment marked a turning point. For the second time, I found myself in a counsellor's sanctuary, seeking solace for a part of me I didn't yet understand. It felt like a much-needed spa treatment for my soul.

Session after session, I began to unravel the patterns that had shaped my life. My counsellor didn't judge or push; she held up a mirror, allowing me to see the cycles I had been trapped in for years. During one of these sessions, she handed me a book, *Women Who Love Too Much* by Robin Norwood.

"You might not be ready for it yet," she said. "Take your time. It's not an easy read but an important one."

She was right. For months, the book sat on my shelf, untouched. I wasn't ready to confront the truths it held. But one quiet evening, I picked it up after my boys had gone to bed. As I turned the pages, it felt like Robin Norwood spoke directly. Her words cracked me open, revealing truths I hadn't dared to confront.

I saw myself in its pages — in the endless giving, fixing, and sacrificing I had mistaken for love. I began to understand that the patterns I had repeated in my relationships weren't random; they were deeply rooted in the wounds of my past. I had unconsciously sought partners who mirrored the dynamics I had grown up with, replaying the same cycles of hurt and longing.

The book didn't just resonate — it changed me. I began to see a way out of the shadows for the first time. Robin Norwood's words illuminated a profound truth: love wasn't meant to deplete me. It wasn't something I had to earn through pain or endurance. True love, I realized, began with loving myself.

As I continued counselling, I delved deeper into the book's lessons. My counsellor helped me unlearn the patterns that had kept me stuck, gently guiding me toward a new way of being. It wasn't easy. Even when it hurts, letting go of the familiar is one of the hardest things to do. But with each session, I felt a little lighter and hopeful.

Looking back now, I see how much of my life was shaped by the shadows of my past. But I also see the light that persisted — the strength I found in those darkest moments, the resilience that carried me forward. *Women Who Love Too Much* was more than a book; it was a guidepost, a reminder that the familiar isn't always safe and that actual growth lies in stepping into the unfamiliar.

Over the years, I've shared this book with many women. Some have embraced its wisdom, finding it as transformative as I did. Others couldn't get through it — it wasn't their time yet. And that's the beauty of this book: it meets you where you are. For me, *Women Who Love Too Much* became a guidepost. It taught me that while the familiar feels safe, proper growth and freedom lie in stepping into the unfamiliar — the new dance steps.

For others, it might remain on a shelf, waiting until they're ready. But when the time is right, it can change lives.

This chapter of my life wasn't the end of my struggles but the beginning of my awakening. Slowly, I began to rebuild — not just my life, but myself. I was learning to believe in the possibility of a life defined not by the shadows but by the light I was slowly cultivating within. The shadows hadn't entirely lifted, but for the first time, I could see cracks of light breaking through.

This wasn't the end of my journey, but it was the start of something new — a path toward balance, healing, and self-discovery.

CHAPTER 3:
The Healing Power of Energy

Skipping through my years in the corporate world, much of the same pattern began to emerge: unhealthy relationships, shadows interspersed with light, and a constant undercurrent of striving yet feeling unfulfilled. Eventually, I made a conscious decision to be on my own. It was easier, less complicated, and, if I'm being sincere, I no longer trusted my judgment regarding love.

So, I threw myself into myself. I embarked on a journey of self-discovery, a reclamation of the parts of myself I had neglected for so long. It began with something as simple—and profound—as getting fit and losing weight.

You know the story: for years, your life revolved around work, children, and everyone else's needs. You drop to the bottom of the priority list somewhere in that mix. Nearing my late forties, I realized the pounds had piled on, my energy was depleted, and my fitness routine was non-existent. Exercise wasn't part of my agenda, let alone my identity.

One day, I looked in the mirror and didn't recognize myself. I wasn't just more significant in size—I was someone I no longer felt connected to. I saw a woman who had given so much to others that she had forgotten how to care for herself. That moment sparked something within me, a quiet determination that it was time for a change.

I found a local personal trainer and began one-on-one sessions with him. At first, it was uncomfortable. My body resisted, and my mind questioned whether I could stick with it. But as the weeks went on, something remarkable began to happen. For the first time in years, I was prioritizing myself. The kids were grown and living their own lives, and I realized there were only so many evenings I could spend sitting at home, letting life pass me by.

When I set my mind to something, I do it wholeheartedly. I immersed myself in this new chapter with laser focus. I signed up for every class I could find, from spinning to Pilates, and within three months, I was fitter, leaner, and more energized than I had been in years. I was glowing, not just physically but from within. It felt like I was rediscovering myself piece by piece.

During this phase of self-care and transformation, I first encountered the power of energy and healing.

It was through my fitness classes that I first heard about a local aromatherapist, well-known for her incredible treatments. In this new chapter of learning to prioritise myself, I eagerly booked an appointment. It felt both indulgent and exciting — a treat not just for the body, but for the soul.

Walking into her treatment room was like stepping into another world. The space felt like a warm, protective cocoon, enveloping me in soft light and soothing scents. From the moment I lay on the couch, it was as if the world's weight had slipped away. A deep sense of peace washed over me — something I hadn't felt in years, maybe decades.

Midway through the treatment, she paused and asked me softly, "Would you like some Reiki?"

Her question startled something in me, stirring memories I had long buried. Reiki. That word was familiar, though I couldn't immediately place why. Something about it felt significant, like an echo from another version of me.

Many years ago, during another crisis at work, I first encountered Reiki healing. At the time, I didn't even know what Reiki was. I was walking down a street, feeling like my world had collapsed again. I had lost my job — a position I had poured my heart and soul into — over a boss who wanted more than I was willing to give, and through errors in my judgment, I found myself unemployed. I was broken, ashamed, and utterly lost. It was much later that I realized shame and guilt were a pattern that I was to play out regularly.

As I wandered, I saw a sign in a shop window that said Reiki Healing. I barely noticed the word "Reiki." All I saw was healing; that word alone felt like a lifeline. I was in desperate need of it.

That first session was unlike anything I had ever experienced. I felt like a dam had burst inside me from the moment it began. I cried with wild abandonment, the kind of uncontrollable sobbing that comes from deep within the soul. At one point during the treatment, an excruciating pain flared in my back, just between my shoulder blades — a physical manifestation of the emotional turmoil I had been carrying. When the session ended, the therapist placed her hand gently on that exact spot and asked me, "Have you been stabbed in the back?"

Her words hit me like a punch to the stomach. I had been stabbed in the back—betrayed by someone I had considered a friend. A colleague I trusted had significantly affected my downfall, contributing to my dignity and job loss. Now, she sat in the very position I had once held. I hadn't fully allowed myself to acknowledge that betrayal's pain until that moment.

I never returned to that therapist. The session had been too intense, too overwhelming. It frightened me, stirring emotions I wasn't ready to confront. Yet, years later, when the aromatherapist during my self-care journey suggested incorporating Reiki into my treatment, I hesitated but ultimately agreed. Tentatively, I opened myself up to the experience once again.

This time, it was different. The energy felt nurturing and soothing, wrapping me in a cocoon of safety and light. As the session unfolded, I saw vibrant colours and vivid images emerge behind my closed eyes. Unlike anything I had felt, a sense of joy and peace washed over me. The therapist moved around me with a natural ease, an intuitive grace that seemed guided by something beyond the physical realm. She could sense exactly what my spirit needed, even when I couldn't articulate it myself.

I was hooked. My curiosity was acutely alert, like a spark igniting a long-dormant fire. This healing and connection felt like I had come home to something I had always known but had somehow forgotten. I wanted to understand it fully, not just experience it but immerse myself in it. I begged her to tell me how to learn and master this gift. I needed to know more to unravel the mystery of this profound energy that had touched me so profoundly.

For those who may not be familiar, Reiki healing is the gentle art of harnessing universal life energy—a profound, infinite force that flows through all living things. At its core, Reiki is a reminder of our innate connection to this energy, ourselves, and the world around us. It invites balance, renewal, and alignment, offering a way to return to wholeness.

The word "Reiki" originates from Japanese, combining rei, meaning "universal" or "spiritual wisdom," with ki, the "vital life energy" that animates us. Together, they represent the harmonizing power of spiritual energy transcending the physical. Reiki is not bound by belief or doctrine; it doesn't demand adherence to any particular system. It simply exists, waiting to flow where it is needed most.

A Reiki session is often profoundly relaxing, as though the body and soul are cradled in a warm, soothing embrace. The practitioner acts as a channel for the universal energy, using their hands to guide its flow to areas where healing is needed. Importantly, this energy doesn't originate from the practitioner—they are merely a conduit, holding space for the recipient to access their innate capacity for healing.

Reiki understands that energy imbalances within the body can manifest as physical, emotional, or spiritual discomfort. These imbalances may stem from unresolved trauma, accumulated stress, or daily life's simple wear and tear. By restoring balance, Reiki encourages the body's natural healing processes to activate, offering a profound sense of clarity and wholeness.

What makes Reiki so extraordinary is its intuitive nature. The energy knows where to go, what to mend, and how to move, even when the recipient may not fully understand their needs. It bypasses the mind's clutter, working on a deeper, more subtle level that resonates with the soul's truths rather than the stories the mind has constructed. It's a form of healing that is gentle and powerful, reminding us of the limitless potential for transformation within each of us.

Reiki has always felt like reconnecting with a forgotten language—one spoken not with words but with energy and intention. It is an invitation to surrender, trust the process, and release the resistance that holds us back from true peace. Perhaps its greatest gift is the reminder that healing isn't about fixing something broken; it's about returning to the essence of who we are. In its quiet, unassuming way, Reiki helps us remember that we are already whole, connected, and deserving of care.

And so, I embarked on my Reiki journey, becoming attuned to Reiki Levels 1 and 2. My first attunement was nothing short of magical. The course began with an introduction to the history of Mikao Usui, the founder of Usui Reiki—a Japanese spiritual teacher born in 1865. His path to discovering Reiki was rooted in a deep curiosity about healing and the mysteries of life energy. A lifelong seeker, Usui explored spiritual disciplines ranging from Buddhism and Shinto to martial arts and energy work. His profound awakening came during a 21-day meditation retreat on Mount Kurama in Japan. Through fasting, prayer, and deep reflection, Usui experienced a connection with the universal energy he named Reiki. This connection provided insights into how this energy could be channelled for healing and spiritual alignment, forming the foundation of the Usui Reiki system. His teachings, passed down with care, continue to touch countless lives worldwide.

The attunement itself was a transformative experience—a sacred ritual facilitated by a Reiki Master to awaken and deepen one's connection to universal life energy. Each person's experience is unique, but mine felt like stepping into a realm beyond this world. I encountered my Reiki guide during the attunement, an ethereal presence of extraordinary beauty. Feminine in form, she radiated a profound warmth that enveloped my entire being. She revealed her name to me: "Amethyst," a name that mirrored her shimmering, tranquil essence. In her presence, I felt a profound sense of peace, a deep belonging, as if I had reunited with a part of myself I didn't realize had been missing. That meeting remains a guiding light in my life, a reminder of the infinite connections that Reiki offers.

From the moment I became Reiki attuned, I knew it would always be a part of me. Just speaking the word seemed to awaken something deep within me — my hands would burn with energy as if eager to channel the universal life force. I practiced at every opportunity, honing my ability to sense when someone needed nurturing and comfort. These early experiences were transformative, teaching me not only the mechanics of Reiki but also the profound, humbling truth of its essence: the ability to help others rebalance, to hold space for their healing, and to serve as a conduit for energy that flows through us all. It was a privilege and a responsibility, and with each session, I felt my connection to Reiki deepen, weaving it ever more firmly into the fabric of my being.

That first step into Reiki opened a new world for me that seemed to expand with every experience. It wasn't long before energy healing led me to the enchanting realm of crystal healing. During a session with the same therapist who had reintroduced me to Reiki, I was drawn to the vibrant array of stones displayed on her windowsill. Their beauty was mesmerizing, each one shimmering with an inner light that seemed to call to me.

Sensing my curiosity, she kindly handed me one to hold. As I cradled it in my palm, I felt an unmistakable sensation — an energetic throb, like a pulsing heartbeat resonating through my hand. It was as though the crystal itself was alive, communicating in a language I was beginning to understand. That moment sparked a fascination that would soon grow into a deep and lasting connection with the power of crystals, their unique energies, and their role in healing and balance.

She told me about a wondrous place called *The Crystal Barn* in Kettering in the heart of the U.K. — a haven of energy and light that had become the heart of crystals in the Midlands. Her voice carried a sense of reverence as she described it, painting a picture of a space brimming with natural beauty and serenity that could only come from being surrounded by the Earth's treasures.

Encouraging me to visit, she promised it would be an experience unlike any other — a journey into a world where the stones seemed to hum with ancient wisdom. Taking her advice, I made the trip, and from the moment I stepped through its doors, I knew I had found something special.

The Crystal Barn isn't just a shop; it is a sanctuary, a place where time seems to pause and where the energy of the crystals envelops you like a warm embrace. To this day, it remains one of my most cherished retreats — a space I return to often to reconnect, recharge, and deepen my love for these remarkable gifts of the Earth.

Nestled in the tranquil countryside, *The Crystal Barn* feels like stepping into another realm. This enchanting sanctuary exudes a sense of serenity from the moment you arrive. The barn has a rustic charm, with wooden beams and soft lighting creating an inviting atmosphere that feels grounded and magical.

Inside the space is a kaleidoscope of colour and energy. Every surface seems to glimmer with the vibrant hues of crystals, arranged thoughtfully in displays that invite exploration. Shelves and tables are adorned with everything from tiny tumblestones to breathtaking clusters and geodes, each radiating its unique energy. The air hums with a quiet vitality, a sense that these stones are more than just beautiful — they are alive with ancient wisdom and healing power.

The staff are warm and knowledgeable, eager to share the stories and properties of each crystal, helping visitors find what speaks to their hearts and needs. Whether you're a seasoned crystal enthusiast or a curious newcomer, *The Crystal Barn* offers an experience that is deeply personal and profoundly calming. It's more than a shop — it's a place where the soul feels nurtured, and the connection to the Earth's energy becomes tangible.

For healing, balance, and growth. The journey begins with something straightforward: choosing a crystal that calls to you. Yes, it's genuinely that intuitive.

For those reading this inclined to venture into the world of crystals, let yourself be guided by your instincts. You might be drawn to a particular colour, texture, or shape — or perhaps you'll hold one in your hand and feel an immediate connection, a sense that you don't want to put it down. That's your crystal. It's as if it has chosen you, aligning its energy with yours, ready to support you on your path. Trust that pull; it's the beginning of a beautiful relationship with the energy of the Earth.

My home is now adorned with beautiful crystals, each one a testament to the journey I've embarked on. They grace my windowsills, shelves, and bedside tables, their vibrant colours and unique forms bringing peace and beauty to every room. Just as I continue to hand out Robin Norwood's *Women Who Love Too Much* to those I feel it might help, I also find myself gifting crystals to friends, family, and even strangers I meet by chance. It's incredible to see how many of these recipients now have their collections — some quite extensive — all radiating healing, love, and nurturing energy into the hands of their new owners.

The relationship with crystals is a partnership, one that requires mutual care. Just as they look after us, we must look after them. Crystals absorb and hold energy, so they need regular cleansing to stay clear and compelling. They thrive when recharged under the sun's light or the moon's glow. There's nothing quite like a full moon to infuse them with renewed energy, as if the universe is nurturing them. I cherish a ritual — a moment of connection between the Earth's gifts and the cosmos, reminding me of the endless flow of energy surrounding and supporting us.

For those who are sceptical, it's worth noting that there is growing scientific interest in the energetic and vibrational properties of crystals. While their healing abilities might not always fit neatly into conventional frameworks, studies in fields like quantum mechanics and vibrational energy have offered intriguing insights. Crystals, by their very structure, are stable, repeating energy patterns. This unique atomic arrangement allows them to absorb, store, and transmit energy in measurable and profound ways.

Quartz, for example, is widely used in technology — from watches to computers — because it generates a precise and stable frequency. If crystals can influence and regulate mechanical systems, it opens the door to understanding how they might interact with the body's energetic systems. Additionally, the placebo effect, which underscores the power of belief and intention, can amplify the experience of working with crystals, aligning the mind and body toward healing and balance.

Whether you view crystals as tools of science, spirituality, or simply symbols of intention, their ability to resonate with us profoundly is undeniable. Sometimes, it's not about "proof" in the traditional sense but about the experience they bring—the feeling of calm, clarity, and connection that so many find when they work with these remarkable gifts from the Earth.

They are a profoundly cherished gift, bringing incredible joy and a profound sense of connection to the world around me.

Reiki and crystals have been more than tools for healing—they have been bridges, reconnecting me to the profound rhythm of nature and the infinite energy surrounding us all. Through Reiki, I learned to listen to my soul's whispers, trust in the flow of universal life force, and find balance within myself. Crystals, with their ancient wisdom and grounding presence, became my companions, teaching me to honour the Earth and the gifts it provides. Together, they nurtured my spirit and helped me heal wounds I thought would never mend. These practices became the foundation of a spiritual journey that continues to unfold, leading me toward greater understanding, peace, and connection. In embracing their energies, I found healing and a path back to my essence—a journey of rediscovery that is as infinite and boundless as the universe.

CHAPTER 4:

Healing and Sisterhood - The Strength to Say No

As a single mother for most of my children's lives, our holidays were a constant—an escape from the demands of everyday life. With the support of my mom and stepdad, we would retreat to a villa in Menorca when the children were little—a haven where we could heal, soak up the sunshine, and be together. It was familiar, comforting, and wrapped in the nurturing arms of my mother.

The sea has always been my solace. Its rhythm calms me, and its vastness humbles me. These holidays became a lifeline, grounding me when life felt overwhelming.

As the children grew older, their needs changed. Gone were the days when a simple beach and sandcastles kept them entertained. Now, food had to be plentiful, gyms were necessary, and flexibility was key. We adapted, shifting to hotels that catered to all of us, embracing this new phase of life.

But, as with all things, this had to end.

In their late teens, with girlfriends in tow, I found myself yet again sitting by the pool alone, wondering what on earth I was doing. My youngest, to this day, teases me about *owing him some holidays*, but at that moment, I knew that enough was enough. It was time to invest in myself. To go on holiday for me, to rest, rejuvenate, and rediscover what I needed.

But where? That was the question.

Traditional *single holidays* held no appeal. They felt forced, unnatural — not me. And yet, as it has so many times before, the universe intervened. It presented me with an opportunity to try something different — an experience that would usher me into a new phase of life.

One evening, flicking through Facebook, I stumbled across a yoga retreat in Ibiza. *Interesting*, I thought, considering I had never actually done yoga. And yet, the pull was undeniable. The flights were short, the setting looked stunning, and most importantly, I would be surrounded by a circle of women who felt familiar, even though I hadn't met them yet.

At the time, I had never flown alone. Now, it's second nature — something I don't even think twice about. But back then, it felt like a big step — a quiet challenge from the universe.

So, I booked it.

I later realized this had become a pattern — jumping into experiences without fully knowing what I was signing up for and following breadcrumbs instinctively, but not yet seeing or understanding why. But the place looked beautiful; I had my room — *what could go wrong?*

Absolutely nothing. And yet, my life changed forever.

For anyone who has never been on a retreat, has experienced some life crisis, or feels lost, please *invest in yourself*. Go on a retreat. They can be life-changing, and for me, this first one altered the course of my life for the better.

Having worked in male-dominated industries all my life, I had always found women to be a conundrum. I naturally gravitated toward male company, finding it easier to connect with them. My experiences with women — aside from my mother — had not been positive ones.

But retreats changed this for me.

A circle of like-minded women is a compelling thing. It's nurturing. It's a haven. And even if you don't connect with everyone, there is something unique and transformative about it.

From the moment I arrived at the retreat, there was an unspoken understanding — a gentle energy that wrapped around me like a warm embrace. I was surrounded by women I had never met, yet there was no awkwardness or need to explain myself. It felt like I had stepped into a sacred space where the walls were invisible, but the safety was undeniable. This was not just a holiday; it was a homecoming.

The women's circle became the heart of the retreat, a space where we shed our titles, roles, and the expectations the world had placed upon us. In that circle, it didn't matter if we were CEOs, teachers, mothers, or free spirits — here, we were simply women, connected by something more profound than words. Some spoke freely, their voices carrying years of wisdom and experience. Others sat in quiet reflection, absorbing the energy of the group. Some laughed, others cried, and none of it felt uncomfortable. There was no need to fix, judge, or compare — just pure acceptance.

For the first time, I truly understood the power of sisterhood. Having spent years navigating male-dominated industries, I had unknowingly built a wall between myself and other women. But in this circle, those walls crumbled. There was no competition, no pretence—just a shared experience of being human, vulnerable, and whole.

This retreat, this circle, changed something within me. It redefined my understanding of female connection, showing me that a woman's strength is not just in her independence but also in her ability to be held, supported, and seen.

Among the many incredible women I met on that retreat, there was one who left a profound and lasting impression on me—our yoga teacher. She wasn't just a guide through poses and breathwork; she was a storyteller, a philosopher, a quiet force of wisdom who seemed to know exactly what words to use and when to use them. Every time she spoke, it was as if she was gently unravelling the complexities of life, revealing truths so simple yet so profound that they stayed with you long after the moment had passed.

One afternoon, after a particularly intense session, I found myself sitting with her, drawn in by how she carried herself—with kindness and an unmistakable strength. I asked her something that had been sitting heavily on my heart for years:

"How do you balance being kind with not being taken advantage of?"

I had spent much of my life believing that kindness meant always saying yes, always being available, and always making room for others—often at the cost of my energy and peace. And yet, here was this woman, radiating warmth and compassion but also a quiet, unshakable certainty about who she was.

She didn't answer right away. Instead, she gave me an example that shifted my perspective in a way I've carried with me ever since.

"Imagine someone asks you to go for coffee," she said. *"You don't want to go. You're tired and need time for yourself, but you say yes anyway because it feels like the kind thing to do. But is it?"*

I nodded, instinctively answering yes because I had always believed that.

She smiled gently and shook her head. *"No, that's not kindness. That's an obligation. True kindness is honesty. True kindness respects both you and the other person. If you don't want to go, then saying yes isn't an act of kindness — it's an act of self-betrayal. And when you betray yourself, resentment follows."*

Her words landed like a revelation.

I had never thought of it that way before. I had spent years confusing self-sacrifice with kindness, believing that to be a good person, I had to constantly pour from my cup, even when it was empty. But she was teaching me — I have since repeated hundreds of times — that kindness isn't just about giving to others; it's also about being kind to yourself.

That simple conversation changed the way I navigated my life. It taught me that setting boundaries is not unkind — it's necessary. When done with honesty and love, saying no is one of the kindest things you can do. It prevents resentment, fosters authenticity, and ensures that when you do say yes, it's from a place of genuine willingness, not quiet resentment.

That retreat, that circle, and that teacher reshaped how I understood connection, not just with others but also with myself.

That conversation with my yoga teacher stayed with me, quietly settling into my mind like a seed waiting to take root. At first, I didn't fully realize how much it would impact me. But the more I reflected on her words, the more I began to see how often I had said yes when I truly meant no—how I usually had ignored my own needs to be "kind."

I started noticing it everywhere.

In friendships where I felt drained but stayed out of loyalty.

In work situations where I took on more than I could handle, I feared disappointing others.

I bent to keep the peace in family dynamics, even when it exhausted me.

Most of all, I saw it in my relationships—how I prioritized others' comfort over my truth, convincing myself that compromise was the same as selflessness.

But now, something had shifted. I couldn't unhear what she had told me.

The first time I put it into practice, it felt strange—almost unnatural. Someone invited me for coffee, and I instinctively reached for my usual response: Of course! But something inside me hesitated. Did I want to go? The truth was, I didn't. I was exhausted, I needed time alone, and saying yes would have been an act of obligation, not kindness.

So, instead, I did something I had rarely done before.

I said, *"Thank you for asking, but I will pass this time. I need some quiet time today."*

I braced myself for guilt, for a wave of anxiety that I had let someone down. But instead, something surprising happened. The world didn't end. They didn't hate me. They said, 'No worries, let's catch up again.' And that was it.

It was liberating.

For the first time, I understood what my yoga teacher had meant. Genuine kindness is honest. It doesn't require self-sacrifice. It was such a simple concept, yet it instantly unraveled years of conditioning.

From that point on, I started making different choices.

I stopped saying yes when I meant no.

I stopped feeling guilty for protecting my energy.

I stopped showing up out of obligation and started showing up because I genuinely wanted to.

And as I did, something incredible happened.

My relationships shifted. The ones built on unbalanced giving and quiet resentment began to fade, making space for deeper, more authentic connections, where I was valued for who I was, not just what I could offer.

At work, I spoke up more. I stopped overextending myself to be seen as reliable and instead focused on what mattered.

In my personal life, I became more straightforward about what I needed and deserved. I recognized that setting boundaries wasn't rejection—it was an act of self-respect. And if someone couldn't accept me 'no,' they were likely only interested in what I could give, not who I was.

That retreat had given me many gifts, but this lesson—the ability to choose myself—truly transformed my life.

I often think back to that conversation, to the quiet wisdom of a woman who likely had no idea how deeply her words would shape my journey. And now, when people ask me about kindness and boundaries, I share her example. I passed on the lesson just as she passed it on to me.

The retreat was never just about yoga. It was a doorway—an initiation into a world of holistic healing that extended far beyond the physical body. Until then, I had always associated wellness with things I could measure: exercise, eating well, and getting enough rest. But here, I was introduced to something more profound, more expansive—healing that touched not just the body but also the mind and spirit.

One evening, we gathered in a dimly lit room, cushions and blankets arranged in a circle. A woman, her presence both calming and commanding, guided us into a sound bath. I had no idea what to expect. I lay down, closed my eyes, and as the first sound of the singing bowls filled the space, I felt something shift within me. The vibrations weren't just sounds—they were sensations moving through my body, stirring emotions I hadn't realized were still there. The tones seemed to unravel layers of tension, dissolving knots of stress and exhaustion that years in the corporate world had buried deep in my muscles.

Then came the gong bath, its resonance deeper, almost primal.

The sound reached parts of me that words never could. I felt energy waves rolling over me, unlocking memories and releasing emotions I had long suppressed. For the first time, I wasn't just thinking about healing—I was feeling it, experiencing it in a way that transcended logic.

For so long, I had been operating on autopilot—balancing the relentless demands of work, motherhood, and life itself, rarely pausing long enough to ask: *Who am I beneath all these roles?* The retreat forced me to slow down, listen, and tune in to a voice I had been ignoring—my own.

It was here that I genuinely understood that healing isn't just about stepping away from the stress of daily life—it's about learning how to integrate peace into it. It wasn't about running away from the corporate grind but about discovering who I was outside of my work, outside of the expectations placed upon me.

For the first time in years, I felt aligned, as though I was no longer just surviving but truly living. The retreat didn't erase all the challenges waiting for me back home, but it gave me something invaluable: a new approach.

Over the next five years, my journey took me to places I had once only dreamed of—Bali, Puglia, Spain, Ibiza, and retreats closer to home in the UK. Each destination carried its unique energy, yet the common thread remained: women coming together, creating space for healing, reflection, and transformation.

Bali was pure magic—the air thick with the scent of incense and frangipani, offerings placed delicately on doorsteps, and the gentle hum of life flowing in perfect harmony. The retreat here was deeply spiritual, woven with ancient Balinese rituals that felt like stepping into another world. It was here that I first truly embraced stillness, learning that healing didn't always come from doing but from being.

Puglia, with its sun-drenched olive groves and slow, deliberate way of life, taught me about simplicity and nourishment, not just in the food (which was divine) but in the way life was lived. Long meals, deep conversations, and an unhurried presence reminded me that healing also comes from allowing ourselves to savour life rather than rush through it.

Spain and Ibiza were different again. The retreats here were vibrant and playful, encouraging movement, dance, and the release of old, stagnant energy. In these places, I truly learned the power of embodiment—of reconnecting with my body, listening to it, and trusting it in ways I never had before.

And then there was the UK, where healing felt raw, grounded, and deeply connected to my roots. In the stillness of countryside retreats, away from the noise of daily life, I found clarity—a reminder that we don't always need to escape far to find ourselves. Sometimes, everything we need is already within reach.

Each retreat had been more than a destination—a lesson, a moment in time that shaped me. With every journey, I peeled back another layer, uncovering who I was beneath the titles, the responsibilities, the expectations. I had finally found balance—I was happy, the fittest I had ever been, armed with new tools for life and thriving in a career I had built with my own hands. What could go wrong?

Yet, as had happened before, all the wisdom, all the healing, and nourishment I had received—I was about to throw away for a relationship.

CHAPTER 5:
Loosing Myself in Love

I remember one particular evening on my Bali retreat, sitting beneath a sky heavy with stars, talking for hours with a beautiful soul from America. She had come to Bali to reevaluate her life, torn between the freedom she cherished and the opportunity to settle down with a man she loved but couldn't quite see fitting into her world.

That night, we dissected every fear, every "what if," every possibility. She kept asking, *What do I have to lose by trying?* As the conversation unfolded, it became clear — what if he was the man of her dreams? What if love wasn't meant to be figured out but experienced?

Somewhere in the early hours of the morning, we made a pact.

"I'll give it a go," she said, *"but only if you do too."*

At the time, I laughed. Love? Relationships? After everything I had been through? I had spent so much time finding myself again, so much energy rebuilding my confidence, sense of worth, and trust in my judgment. The idea of risking all that for another relationship seemed absurd.

But true to her word, she kept her promise. She gave love a chance, and months later, when she reached out to check on me, she called me out.

"Well? I did my part. Have you?"

I hadn't.

And so, with a mix of curiosity and hesitation, I decided to step back into the dating world. This time, though, things would be different. This time, I would trust myself.

And that's how I met my next partner—through those dreaded dating apps.

This time, indeed, I wouldn't make the same mistakes. This time, I would trust my judgment.

When I met him, it felt like stepping into warmth after years in the cold. I had been on my own for so long—seven years without a single date, without so much as a touch, without the quiet comfort of simply being beside someone. I hadn't realized how much I had missed the simple things.

The softness of a hand on mine, the familiar weight of someone beside me on the sofa, the casual intimacy of sharing stories at the end of a long day. Even the mundane moments—grocery shopping together, laughing at something silly on the television, the way he instinctively reached for my hand—felt like things I had been starved of without even knowing it.

And so, I fell. Quickly. Completely. Or at least, I thought I had.

There were red flags I chose to ignore.

I had spent years learning, healing, and growing, and yet, somehow, all of it seemed to vanish when love came knocking. Looking back, I see it now — the red flags were there from the start. But I ignored them, excusing them as quirks, signs of deep affection, proof that he cared.

One moment still lingers in my mind.

I had been on the road all day, bouncing between meetings, my phone tucked away in my bag. When I finally checked it, I saw the missed calls — several from friends, a few from work, and one from him, followed by a message: Where are you?

I didn't think much of it. I called him back when I had a moment, expecting an easy conversation. But what I got instead was a sharp telling-off.

"Where the hell have you been?" he snapped, his voice edged with frustration.

"Why didn't you answer your phone? I've been worried sick — you could be dead!"

I laughed it off, dismissing his words as dramatic. How ridiculous, I thought. But still, something in his tone — not concern, but control — made my stomach twist.

I didn't like being spoken to like that. I told him as much. He got the firm end of my tongue, and for a brief moment, I felt like I had set a boundary. But then I let it pass.

I should have listened to my gut feeling.

I should have heard the undercurrent of control in his words, the need to track my every move, the desire to mould me into something more manageable, more available, less independent.

But I didn't.

I ignored the warning bells because I wanted to believe in love. I tried to think I had finally found someone to share my life with, someone to fill the spaces that had felt empty for so long.

And so, I stayed. Not only did I wait, but I also let him move into my home. My space—once a sanctuary I had built—was now ours. We tried to coexist, blend our lives together, and make it work.

It didn't end well.

For a variety of reasons, we eventually went our separate ways. But not for long.

I didn't realize it at the time, but I had another pattern running in the background—one I had been blind to for years. I was always trying to save people.

I see it clearly now, but it was second nature back then. If someone was hurting, I wanted to heal them. If they were lost, I tried to guide them. If they were struggling, I wanted to fix things for them—even if it came at my own cost.

And so, despite knowing we weren't right for each other, I tried to save him.

I suggested counselling—to me, it was like a spa treatment for the mind, a safe way to understand yourself, unravel your past, and build something better. And he had a few things to resolve.

To my relief, he agreed. He went to counselling and seemed to be a changed man. Communication improved, thoughtfulness restored, and we were suddenly happy again. I convinced myself we had turned a corner.

Then COVID hit—and in truth, it was terrific.

We created the illusion of happiness.

We were wrapped in an isolated bubble, a world just for the two of us. We spent hours together, talking and walking, sharing honest, deep, and meaningful moments. There was nowhere to rush to, no outside world demanding our time, no distractions pulling us apart.

It wasn't until later that I understood *why* I felt so happy, *why* that time had been so fulfilling.

I had since read a life-changing book—*The Five Love Languages*—and suddenly, everything made sense. My love language is quality time. Talking, sharing, just being together fills me up, making me feel safe, wanted, and deeply loved. And that's precisely what COVID has given me. It forced us into a space where time was all we had, and I thrived in it.

But I didn't realize that his love language wasn't the same as mine.

This house was meant to be our forever home.

As restrictions lifted, so did his need for space. The closeness I had cherished wasn't what he needed, and I could feel the shift. We tried to move forward and evolve into the next phase, so we agreed to look at buying a house together.

I already had my home—beautifully furnished, exactly as I had wanted—but he had been renting and longed for stability. I understood that.

So, I agreed to sell, but on one condition—we would have land.

COVID had taught me something deeply personal—I needed nature. I had spent too many years locked in offices, trapped in routines that pulled me away from the things that genuinely balanced me. I longed to be outside, connected to the land, and create a space where I could find peace amidst the chaos of my working life.

We found our dream home. It had land, potential, and everything I thought we both wanted. And so, I threw myself into it, pouring love into the house, the garden, and the foundation of what I believed would be our future.

But I didn't realize—I couldn't see—how jealous he would become of that love.

I had assumed we were building something together. For me, love was in the moments spent side by side—gardening together, chopping down trees, cutting back hedgerows. It was creating, nurturing, and growing—not just a home but a life.

But I didn't realize—I couldn't see—that wasn't his language.

Instead of seeing my love and devotion, he saw my attention drifting away. Instead of recognizing my joy in creating something for us, he saw me as lost in a world that didn't include him.

We weren't speaking the same language, and it was only a matter of time before we stopped hearing each other.

At first, it felt like love. That's how it always begins — a quiet compromise here, a small sacrifice there. Until one day, you wake up and realize you're no longer the person you used to be.

The truth is, he never stopped me from doing anything — I chose it. I decided to spend less time on my yoga mat, not because he asked me to, but because I craved connection more than my own space. I wanted to be loved and wanted and feel that sense of belonging. And so, without realizing it, I started putting us first, above the things that had once brought me balance.

He loved his own time. He had his golf, his solo pursuits, his space. He never questioned making time for them and felt the need to justify it. On the other hand, I constantly weighed my choices against the time we could spend together. Instead of rolling out my yoga mat in the mornings, I lingered in bed because that's where he was. Instead of escaping into silence to reconnect with myself, I stayed close to him because I wanted to feel connected to someone.

And then there was the house.

I've always loved creating a home, adding beauty to my space, and making it warm and inviting. But to him, those things felt unnecessary. He didn't see the point. He was not against it — he didn't understand it. *"Why are you wasting money on that?"* he'd ask when I talked about something as simple as a new cushion, a candle, or a fresh coat of paint.

Yet, there was no hesitation when it came to the things he valued — his golf clubs, his equipment, the things that mattered to him. He never questioned spending money on those. But the idea of spending money on a candle? That was a waste.

It wasn't about the money. It was about what we valued and how differently we saw the things that brought us joy.

At first, I brushed it off, convincing myself it was just a personality difference. But over time, I realized it was more than that — a disconnect between what made me feel alive and what made him feel alive. And instead of holding onto the things that brought me joy, I let them go.

Not because he asked me to. Because I thought it would make love feel safer.

I had spent many years searching for balance, self-awareness, and a life that aligned with who I was. And yet, here I was again, abandoning myself piece by piece to keep love alive.

Why do women lose themselves ?

Why do we do this? Why do so many women — strong, independent, self-sufficient women slowly shrink themselves in relationships? Why do we stop doing what we love, compromise our happiness, and convince ourselves that love requires sacrifice?

I didn't realize I was doing it at the time. It was never one big decision, never an outright choice to lose myself. It happened in small, almost imperceptible ways — choosing time with him over my yoga practice, deferring to his opinions about what mattered, and adjusting my rhythm to fit his. It didn't feel like I was initially giving up parts of myself. It just felt like love.

As women, we are taught that love is about giving. We grow up watching women who compromise, adjust, and accommodate, making themselves smaller so relationships can survive. We inherit this unspoken belief that to love is to put others first—to create space, to be flexible, to nurture, to heal, to fix.

I wasn't forced to give anything up—I gave it up willingly because I wanted love to feel safe.

And then there's the other pattern that runs just as deep.

Why do we always believe that we can save our partners?

Maybe it's instinct, perhaps it's conditioning, or maybe it's the belief we carry that love can fix what's broken. Somewhere along the way, we learn that if a man is emotionally unavailable, struggles to express love, is distant, resistant, or afraid, we can love him into healing.

We believe that he will eventually see if we are patient enough, understanding enough, and giving sufficient. He will soften. He will meet us in the space we have been holding for him.

And so, we wait.

We forgive.

We try harder.

We convince ourselves that he needs time, support, and us to show him what love looks like.

But here's what I've learned — the hard way:

You cannot love someone into being who you need them to be.

You cannot pour your energy into saving someone who does not want to be saved. You cannot force someone to value what you value, no matter how much you believe in them or how much you give.

I could make him see the beauty in what I loved — creating a home, cherishing small things, and carving out moments of connection that felt intentional and real. But he didn't see it. He didn't want to see it.

And instead of recognizing that we weren't aligned, I did what so many of us do — I tried to bend myself to fit him.

I didn't demand that he step up and meet me where I was — I slowly stepped down to meet him where he was.

And by the time I realized it, I had given away far too much of myself.

There's a saying: "You are the average of the six people you spend the most time with." I used to think this was just another self-help cliché, something motivational speakers throw around. But when I look back, I see how painfully true it is.

We don't always consider how the people around us shape, drain, or change us. We think we are independent, that we make our own choices, that we are in control of who we become. But without realizing it, we absorb the energy of those closest to us — their habits, beliefs, and ways of seeing the world.

And I had done just that.

Oh, I had friends who saw it before I did. One in particular tried to tell me — she saw the shift, the slow erosion of the positivity I had worked so hard to cultivate. She told me my energy was drained and that I wasn't the same light-filled person I had been before.

And yet, I chose to ignore it.

Because that's the thing about love: we convince ourselves that it's just a phase, that it's not as bad as it seems, and that all relationships require sacrifice. We excuse the small losses, telling ourselves that they don't matter — until we wake up one day and realize we don't even recognize ourselves anymore.

And then yet again the universe intervenes.

But here's the thing about the universe — it has a way of bringing you back to the lessons you refuse to learn. And when you ignore them long enough, it doesn't whisper — it smacks you in the face.

For me, that moment came in a way I never expected.

My partner had a family crisis, something harrowing and life-altering. It shook everything. It reminded us of life's fragility, how short our time truly is, and how we take things for granted until they are suddenly ripped away.

And in the aftermath of that pain, he made a decision.

He left.

Just like that, the man I had bent myself to fit, the man I had tried to build a forever home with, the man I was engaged to marry — was gone.

At the time, I was heartbroken. I couldn't understand it. How could this be happening? How could he walk away after everything we had built? Hadn't we planned a future together? Hadn't we fought for this?

I was left staring at the life we had started to create — the home, the engagement, the dreams we had woven together — and suddenly, it meant nothing.

But here's the part I couldn't see then — the part that makes perfect sense now.

The universe wasn't punishing me. It was saving me.

Because, in reality, I hadn't lost my future — I had just been handed back my freedom.

At the time, I thought I had lost everything.

I had spent years convincing myself that love required patience, sacrifice, and understanding — if I just gave more, tried harder, and held on longer, everything would work out. And yet, in the end, it was he who walked away.

I remember sitting in the house — the one we had planned as our forever home — surrounded by everything that was supposed to represent us: the engagement ring, the furniture we had chosen together, and the garden I had lovingly poured myself into.

And suddenly, it all felt empty.

The man I had shaped my life around was gone, and I was left with nothing but the question: *Who am I without this relationship?*

I felt blindsided, lost, and heartbroken. I couldn't understand how something that had felt so certain could unravel completely. Hadn't we fought for this? Hadn't we built something real?

But here's the thing about the universe—it doesn't operate on sentimentality. It doesn't care about the plans you made in your head. It only cares about what is true.

And the truth was, I wasn't losing my future.

I was being handed back my freedom.

It was my opportunity to reclaim my life and my home.

I ended up buying the house from him. It wasn't a pleasant exercise—far from it. There were negotiations, tension, and the pain of untangling two lives that were never meant to be entirely woven together.

For a while, it felt like a hollow victory. This house was now mine, but instead of feeling like an accomplishment, it felt like a reminder of everything that had fallen apart.

But then, as the months passed, something began to shift.

Without his presence, the house no longer held the heavy energy of compromise. Slowly, room by room, I reclaimed it. I filled the spaces with things that made me happy—not things I had to justify or defend. I bought the candles, cushions, flowers, and small things that once made me feel at home. With each change, I felt a piece of myself returning.

I had a stressful, demanding career as a Managing Director. I had built a life on my terms, with financial stability, independence, and the ability to create a home that was truly mine. But somewhere along the way, I had convinced myself that nothing meant anything without someone to share it with.

I see it differently now.

Losing him wasn't about losing myself, it was about finding me again.

I hadn't just repurchased a house.

I had repurchased my peace.

I had repurchased my voice.

I had repurchased my freedom.

And in the end, I realized something even more powerful: I had never needed to be saved.

I just needed to stop saving everyone else and finally choose me.

CHAPTER 6:
Losing Myself in Work – The Distraction of Busyness

The silence after he left was deafening.

I had spent so long trying to make the relationship work, bending, shifting, compromising — until nothing was left to bend for one day. The house was mine; our planned future was gone, and I was utterly alone with myself for the first time in a long time.

And that terrified me.

So, I did what I knew best.

I immersed myself in work.

It was easy to justify. After all, I had a successful career as a Managing Director, leading teams, making big decisions, and constantly moving forward. Work had always been my space of certainty, achievement, and structure — and now, more than ever, I needed something to anchor me.

But I didn't realize then that I wasn't just working hard — I was hiding.

I filled every hour, every moment, with tasks, meetings, deadlines, and decisions because as long as I was busy, I didn't have to sit in the quiet and face what was underneath—the grief, the exhaustion, the profound realization that I had lost myself—not just in love but in life.

Busyness became my shield, and productivity became my coping mechanism. Yet, no matter how much I worked or how many successes I racked up, there was still an emptiness that nothing seemed to fill.

But work wasn't just an escape—I had poured my heart into it for years.

In 2019, I helped bring this business to life, creating something that wasn't just another corporate machine but a place where people could be themselves. I had always believed that if we allowed people to show up as their best, most authentic selves—free from rigid expectations and outdated structures—our clients would get the best from them, too.

And we did just that. Alongside my joint MD, I had built a business that genuinely meant something—a place where people could thrive, where innovation and individuality weren't just encouraged—they were the foundation of our success.

I was proud of what we had built. It had purpose, direction, and impact. It wasn't just a job—it was part of me.

But, as with all things, change was inevitable.

When the business started to change, so did I.

The business was shifting. As the industry evolved and outside pressures mounted, the culture I had worked so hard to create started to change as we grew. There were new demands, new challenges, and new expectations. The company was moving in directions I hadn't entirely foreseen, and suddenly, I found myself in a position I had never been in before—questioning if this was still where I belonged.

Yet instead of stopping to reflect, reassess, and ask myself what I truly wanted, I did what I had always done—I worked harder.

More hours, commitment, and energy were thrown into a business that was no longer the same as the one I had helped create.

I told myself I was okay. This was just another phase of growth, another period of transition. But deep down, I could feel a quiet disconnect starting to take root.

And yet, I ignored it.

Because as long as I was working, fixing problems, leading teams, and making decisions, I didn't have to face the truth.

I had built a business that allowed people to be their best selves—but somehow, I had lost sight of who I was in the process.

Work wasn't filling the void in my life anymore.

I have always believed that success should feel good and that building something meaningful brings fulfillment, purpose, and pride.

But now, even as the business continued to grow, as we hit milestones and achieved the results many would envy, something felt off.

I kept distracting myself with busyness, thinking that if I just did more, achieved more, and worked harder, I would eventually feel whole again.

But that's the thing about using work as an escape—it doesn't heal you. It just keeps you occupied.

And deep down, I knew I couldn't keep running from myself forever.

Something had to change.

I didn't know what that was yet.

Then the economy started to shift and so did everything else.

At first, it was subtle—just small changes, shifts in the market, signs that the economic landscape was tightening. But soon, the challenges became very real, very fast. Budgets were cut, clients hesitated, and the once-thriving momentum of the business felt like it was being chipped away, piece by piece.

And with every challenge, an old pattern I thought I had mastered began resurfacing.

I had spent years working on myself, learning to set boundaries, stop over-giving, and recognize when something was beyond my control. I had promised myself I would never fall into the same trap again—the trap of thinking I could fix everything if I just worked harder, gave more, and pushed through.

And yet, there I was.

I believed that if I just held everything together and poured enough of myself into the business, I could save it.

So, I did what I had always done—I threw myself into the work. I worked longer hours, attended more meetings, and was more profound in every detail. If someone needed support, I was there. If a problem arose, I would find a way to fix it. If morale dropped, I would hold the team's weight on my shoulders.

I told myself it was temporary, just a phase, that soon things would stabilize, and I could breathe again.

But deep down, I knew the truth—I wasn't just trying to save the business. I was trying to save everyone in it.

Because that's what I do, what I've always done.

I had built this company believing in people over processes, creating an environment where everyone could thrive, where they weren't put into boxes and could be their best selves. I had seen what we had built together and refused to let it slip away.

So, I carried more. Gave more. Pushed harder.

And in doing so, I ignored every sign that I was slipping into old habits.

I felt exhausted, overwhelmed, and slowly eroding the balance I had once worked so hard to achieve.

I told myself it was fine, that this was what leadership looked like, and that this was my responsibility.

But at what cost? Because, yet again, I was saving everyone but myself.

CHAPTER 7:
The Call to Something Deeper

Yet again, Facebook and the universe conspired to lead me where I needed to go.

I had fallen out of love with yoga. The practice that had once been my grounding force, escape, and lifeline had become something I avoided. It wasn't because I no longer believed in its power—I did. But my ego wouldn't let me return to it.

I couldn't bear the thought of rolling out my mat and being unable to do the things I had once done with ease. The fluidity, the strength, the grace I had built over the years—what if it wasn't there anymore? What if I had lost it?

But deep down, I wasn't just craving movement.

I was craving connection.

I longed for the safety of a women's circle again, the sacred space where I could be seen, held, and fully myself. I wanted new experiences that would challenge, awaken, and shake me from the numbness of routine.

I needed something more than just a retreat.

And so, almost instinctively, I booked the Goddess Retreat in Zanzibar.

However, calling it a "retreat" felt like an understatement—as though the word itself couldn't quite capture what I was about to experience. This wasn't just an escape from life. This was a journey back to myself.

It was stepping into the unknown.

It felt indulgent.

It felt reckless.

It felt like exactly what I needed.

Because deep down, I knew—this wasn't just a break. It was a homecoming.

I was to learn yet again that the universe will always test you.

Getting to the retreat tested my patience, my emotions, and, more than anything, my faith that things work out exactly as they are meant to.

It started with a delayed flight, leaving me panicking mid-air about connecting in Doha. I couldn't sit still. My mind raced through all the scenarios—*Would I make it? Would I be stuck? Would this whole retreat fall apart before it even began?* Fear, I now know, is another one of my patterns.

Each time I asked, the flight attendants reassured me. *"It will be fine. Someone will meet you when we land."*

But that didn't happen.

As soon as we touched down, I bolted off the plane, my heart pounding as I raced toward the transfer desk. Deep down, I already knew — I wouldn't make it.

And I was right.

"I'm sorry, Miss. You won't get your connection flight."

Her words hit me like a brick wall. Exhaustion, frustration, and panic all surged to the surface at once. Now what?

To this day, I don't know what made me do it, but I switched on my phone at that exact moment.

I received a sign from the universe.

Now, let me remind you — I was in Doha in a completely different time zone in the middle of the night. Who was I even expecting to call? I had no idea what I was doing.

But the second I turned my phone on, it rang immediately.

I answered breathlessly.

"Miss Tina, we are waiting for you."

I could have collapsed right there.

I started crying with frustration. They were waiting for me — *but I wasn't there! I couldn't get to them in time!* And if you know Doha Airport, you'll understand — it is enormous. Getting from one terminal to another can take ages, and I was already too late.

In front of me stood a young security guard. In a complete state of desperation, I shoved my phone at him and managed to sob, *"Help!"*

I must have looked entirely helpless because he immediately sprang into action.

He rushed me across the terminal straight to the principal security officer, and through actual tears, I begged him to help me.

At first, he hesitated. But then, something shifted.

Rather than dealing with a tearful, stranded passenger, he said: *"Follow me."*

And just like that, I was running after him through Doha Airport.

Through another security check. I took a train to the right terminal through two shopping malls.

I was struggling to breathe—I'm not the fittest person, and sprinting through an airport with a backpack wasn't ideal—but I kept running.

For the Second Time, Someone Was Waiting For Me

As I stumbled down an escalator, **gasping for air**, a woman's voice called out:

"Miss Tina"! For the second time today, *"We are waiting for you."*

I could have hugged her.

I gasped out a thousand apologies as she ushered me forward, but I barely had time to process what was happening before I was put onto another bus — for a 15-minute ride to the plane.

And then came the final moment of shame and joy rolled into one — boarding that plane, knowing it had waited for me for 45 minutes. I was the reason for the delay.

But did I care?

Not one bit.

Because I had made it.

Because the universe had saved me.

Because this journey — the one that was about to change everything — was meant to happen.

I had made the flight. Against all odds, against the ticking clock, against every logistical nightmare that should have stopped me — somehow, I had made it. As I stood at the luggage carousel in Zanzibar, waiting for my suitcase to appear, my worst nightmare unfolded before me.

The other passengers grabbed their bags and moved on, one by one. The crowd thinned. The belt kept moving, but my suitcase was nowhere to be seen. Panic set in. I rushed to the customer service desk, already dreading what they would say.

And then, as if the universe had planned this entire sequence of events to mess with me, the young man behind the desk looked at me calmly and said:

"Miss Tina, we know about your case. It will arrive tomorrow."

I stared at him. *Tomorrow? Tomorrow?*

I wanted to cry.

I had raced through Doha, sprinted through terminals, and thrown myself onto that plane—only to arrive in Zanzibar with nothing but the clothes on my back. The pattern of the fear of not being prepared surfaced.

Now, to some people, lost luggage is an inconvenience. A minor disruption. But to me? This was a trigger. A deep, gut-wrenching, heart-pounding trigger.

For years, I had told myself I would become a better packer—that I wouldn't bring my entire wardrobe for a week-long trip and would stop stuffing my suitcase with 'just in case' outfits.

But here's the truth.

It was never about the clothes; it was about control, about the fear of not being prepared, of standing out when I wanted to blend in, of not having what I needed, of looking out of place, of being talked about, of getting it wrong.

That suitcase wasn't just filled with dresses, sandals, and skincare. It was filled with a safety net; now, the universe had stripped me of it.

I took a deep breath. What choice did I have?

I had two options:

- Let this ruin the start of my journey—spiral into frustration, let the fear of not having enough consume me, and spend the first 24 hours of this retreat worrying about what I didn't have instead of embracing where I was.

- Trust that this was part of the lesson — that this experience, as awful as it felt, was teaching me something I had long resisted.

To let go.

To surrender.

To understand that I am enough, exactly as I am, without the things I bring with me.

So, I exhaled.

"Okay," I told the young man, forcing a smile. *"Tomorrow, then."*

And with that, I walked out into the warm Zanzibar air, carrying nothing but the weight of a lesson I didn't know I needed to learn.

Stepping out of the airport, the warm Zanzibar air wrapped around me, thick with the scent of spice and sea. I had only my handbag and the clothes I had been wearing for nearly 24 hours. My suitcase — my carefully packed safety net — was somewhere else, floating in transit, entirely beyond my control. I felt exposed, unsettled, and not how I imagined my arrival.

And then, I met **Cindy Lobo**.

She stood there, radiating a quiet confidence, grounding, and effortless presence. She took one look at me — flustered, exhausted, processing the reality that I had nothing but the essentials — and instead of offering empty reassurances, she smiled.

"Don't worry," she said calmly, as if this was the most straightforward problem in the world to solve. "We can get you something to wear in Stone Town. We're heading there to meet another guest for a drink."

Just like that, the tension in my chest softened.

There was no drama, over-concern, or fuss—just a simple, practical solution and a reassurance that everything would be fine. And in that moment, I believed her.

I didn't know it then, but this was Cindy—a woman who would change my life over the next year in ways I never could have predicted. For now, though, she was simply the first person to remind me that not everything needed to be controlled and that sometimes, the best thing to do was go with it. And so, instead of spiraling into panic, I exhaled, let go, and followed her.

As we drove towards Stone Town, I felt the weight of the past 24 hours begin to shift. The stress, the exhaustion, the missing suitcase—none of it seemed as important now. Outside the window, Zanzibar unfolded before me, a place unlike anywhere I had ever been. The streets were alive, humming with the energy of a city that felt deeply historic and effortlessly modern. Narrow alleyways wove through grand, old buildings—some weathered and worn by time, others bursting with life, colour, and movement. The air was thick with the scent of spices, grilled seafood, and something sweet I couldn't quite place.

It was a completely different environment from what I was used to—chaotic yet calm, unfamiliar yet welcoming, full of contrasts but overflowing with beauty and then there was the colour.

Everywhere I looked, I was met with bold, vibrant shades—turquoise blues, deep oranges, golden yellows, rich magentas. Clothes hanging in market stalls, walls painted in bright pastels, patterned fabrics draped over balconies. Colour wasn't just present here — it was celebrated.

Which, of course, brought us to my next lesson.

I tend never to wear colour or patterns.

I know — it's limiting, but for as long as I can remember, my wardrobe has been a sea of neutrals — white, cream, black, grey, and navy. Perhaps it reflected my life, of how I had played it safe, staying within the familiar, the comfortable.

So now, I was standing in a place that radiated vibrancy, where colour was stitched into the fabric of life — and I was looking for a white or cream dress.

Cindy, of course, found this hilarious — though she was far too subtle to laugh outright. Instead, she watched with quiet amusement, offering the occasional bemused smile as I sifted through market stalls, determined to find something safe.

"You know," she finally said, as I clung to the one white dress we could find, *"maybe it's time to bring a little colour into your life."*

At the time, I brushed off her comment. It was just a dress, after all — just a preference. But looking back, I see it for what it was — Cindy's first, gentle push.

Because colour isn't just about what we wear; it's about how we live. At that moment, I had no idea how much Cindy was about to bring colour into my life — in ways far beyond what I chose to wear.

By the time we left Stone Town, the last of my tension had begun to unravel. My suitcase was still missing, my dress was the only pale thing in a world of rich, vibrant hues, and I had spent the evening navigating the unknown — yet, somehow, I felt lighter than I had in months. The road opened up as we drove along the coast, revealing glimpses of the ocean — my healing place. The sight of it, vast and endless, was enough to quiet the last remnants of anxiety that still clung to me.

And then, we arrived.

The retreat space was breathtaking — a beautiful, traditional timber villa standing gracefully against the backdrop of nature, just a stone's throw from the ocean. The soft hum of waves filled the air, blending seamlessly with the rustling of palm trees in the warm night breeze. Stepping inside, I felt an instant shift. This was no ordinary place. This was sacred.

I was led to my room, and the moment I stepped in, I knew — everything was exactly as it was meant to be. Laying out on my bed was a gift — a beautiful but colorful sarong. It was soft, lightweight, and utterly unlike anything I would normally wear. This was another invitation from the universe, another nudge toward embracing colour, embracing change, and embracing something new.

And beside it, something even more unexpected — an oracle deck. Not just any deck, but *The Rose Oracle* by Rebecca Campbell. The rose — the ultimate symbol of the feminine. The emblem of softness and strength, surrender and resilience.

I ran my fingers over the box, feeling its weight — not just in my hands but in my heart. This was no coincidence. This was a message, an initiation, a moment designed just for me.

I lay on the bed, feeling the weight of everything that had happened over the past 48 hours. The panic of almost missing my flight, the lesson in letting go when my suitcase didn't arrive, the colour that seemed to be creeping into my life, whether I wanted it to or not.

I traced my fingers over the oracle deck beside me — the rose, the emblem of the feminine. It felt symbolic as if the universe had orchestrated every moment leading up to this point to prepare me for what was coming next. The journey had tested me. It had pushed me into discomfort, stripped me of my illusions of control, and forced me to ask for help, trust, and surrender, and now, finally, I was here.

I listened to the rhythmic hum of the waves, the soft rustling of the trees outside, and the distant sounds of laughter and conversation from the other women who had already begun settling in. For the first time in a long time, I exhaled utterly. I didn't know what the next few days would bring. I only knew something within me was about to shift because I hadn't just come here to rest.

I had come here to awaken.

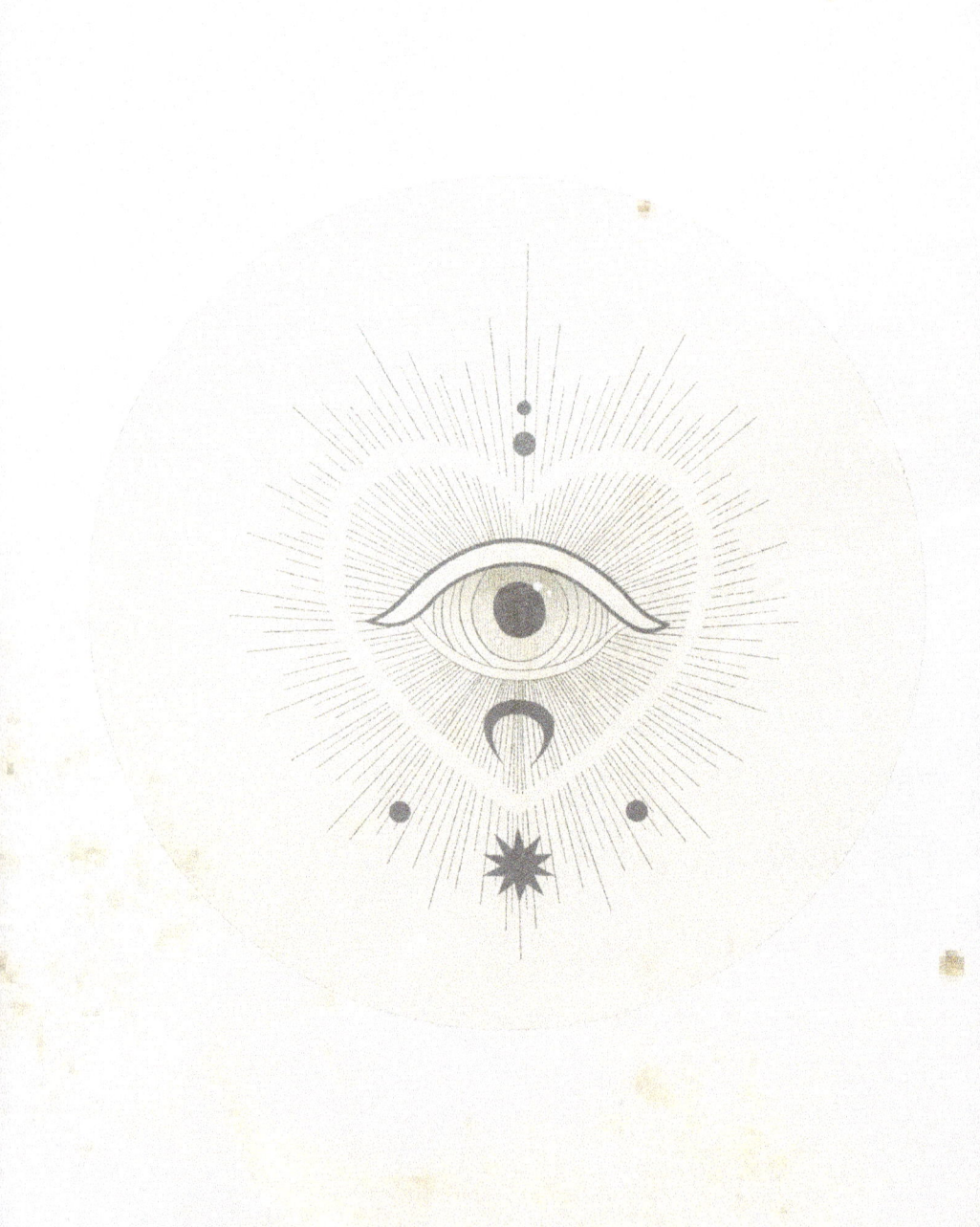

CHAPTER 8:

Reawakening the Goddess – A Journey Back to Myself

As the days unfolded, the retreat became its world, a sacred bubble of feminine energy where time slowed and everything felt intentionally woven together — the ocean's rhythm, the warmth of the air, the quiet moments between us.

There was something undeniably powerful about being surrounded by women, all on their journeys yet connected in ways we couldn't quite explain. It was a space where masks were left at the door, where no one needed to be anything other than exactly who they were.

And at the centre of it all was Cindy.

She didn't lead in the traditional sense, yet she held everything together effortlessly. She held space for all of us, not by dictating or directing, but simply by being there — calm, open, grounded. Then there were the moments she would appear beside you in the most casual, effortless way.

A quiet conversation by the pool.

A gentle check-in over morning tea.

A passing comment as we walked barefoot across the sand.

And yet, every time she spoke, it was as if she was pulling something straight from your soul, exposing the exact thing you needed to hear. Sometimes, her words hit like a punch to the stomach, forcing you to see something you had been avoiding. Other times, they unlocked something so profound inside you that all you could do was sit with it, let it rise, let it open you bare.

No force. No judgment.

Just truth.

The kind of truth that doesn't come from thinking. The type of truth that comes from remembering.

The more time I spent in this space, the more I felt the shift happening within me, and I wasn't just attending a retreat. I was stepping into something ancient, primal, and deeply feminine, with the softness of shared laughter, morning opening of the circles, rituals, and stories exchanged under the stars. There was an awareness of tears shed in the circle, old wounds surfacing, and finally feeling safe enough to let go — the strength of women holding women, eyes locking in silent understanding and unspoken healing.

I had been craving this without knowing it. It wasn't just about the rest of the time away; it was a homecoming to myself that would profoundly change me.

Over the next two days, we stepped into something sacred, ancient, and deeply transformative—the 7 Nusta Karpay initiations. In truth, I had no idea what it was about, what I would learn through the process, or just how much this ritual would shift something inside me.

The Nusta Karpay—the seven initiations of the Andean Goddess energies—are a gift from the Q'ero lineage of Peru, a blessing of feminine wisdom, balance, and healing.

This wasn't just a ceremony. It was a passage through deep layers of the self—through fears, wounds, and forgotten parts of me—and ultimately, a passage back to wholeness. All of us were touched and deeply loved as each initiation carried its energy, lesson, and mirror.

Some were soft and nurturing, like a whisper from a mother's embrace. Some were wild and fierce, demanding that we step fully into our power, and some were so deep and raw that they cracked something open inside me that I hadn't even realized was closed. With each blessing, each energetic transmission, I felt a shift. A clearing. A remembering.

There were moments when I resisted, moments when the energy felt too big, too strong, too much. Tears came without warning, and I didn't even know what I was crying for—only that something was being released, something old, something I no longer needed to carry. Then, there were moments of pure surrender, where I felt myself dissolve into something more significant.

Into the earth beneath me.

Into the wind moving through the trees.

Into the ancient wisdom that had existed long before me and would continue long after.

I wasn't just receiving the initiations. I was becoming them, and by the time we completed the final blessing, I knew something had shifted permanently. I couldn't quite put it into words yet, but I felt it—a deeper softness, a deeper strength, a deeper knowing. It was as if parts of me that had been fragmented were finally coming back together. This wasn't just about the ceremonies. This was about me stepping into the fullness of who I was always meant to be.

Of all the Nusta Karpay initiations, Maria Sakapana shook me the most. The Goddess of the winds and storms, Maria Sakapana, represents the voice—not just the ability to speak but the power to express, to be heard, and to claim space in the world. As the initiation began, I felt something stir inside me, something I hadn't expected.

At first, it was just a sensation—a tightness in my throat, a pressure that built as if something long buried was trying to rise. And then, the realization hit me. Over the years, my voice had shrunk—not in a sudden, dramatic way, but in small, almost imperceptible moments.

I realized that in relationships, I had compromised. I had softened my edges, quietened my needs, and made myself smaller so I wouldn't be "too much." I had dismissed my intuition, brushed aside my concerns, and convinced myself that keeping the peace was more important than speaking my truth.

At work, I had given too much of myself; I had fought to create a business where people could be themselves—but somewhere along the way, I had lost parts of myself in the process. My opinions were valuable, and my insights sharp, but I had stopped pushing too hard and fully stepped into the leader I was meant to be.

Even in my personal life, I had played it safe. I wore neutral colours, kept my emotions in check, and lived within comfortable lines. I had let others speak first, let others decide, and let others lead, and now, here I was, standing in a sacred space under the vast open sky, with Maria Sakapana demanding that I stop silencing myself.

As Cindy guided us through the initiation, the energy became almost unbearable. The winds picked up around us as if the goddess had arrived, stirring everything trapped inside me for years. Tears came before words. A deep, gut-wrenching release that I didn't fully understand, and then, for the first time in a long time — I spoke.

Not just words but a truth that had been suffocating inside me.

A truth that said:

I am done making myself smaller.

I am done filtering myself for the comfort of others.

I am done believing that my voice does not matter.

As I spoke these words, the wind howled around me as if Maria Sakapana herself was answering. You are heard, and by the time the initiation ended, I knew I had changed. I could feel it in my throat, in my chest, in my entire being. Maria Sakapana had come for me, not just to awaken my voice but to remind me that it was never truly gone. I had forgotten how to use it, but now?

The morning after the initiations, I felt different — more rooted, open, and myself than I had in years. But as the retreat continued, life, as it always does, tested this newfound strength.

In our next sharing circle, we gathered as we always did, wrapped in the quiet intimacy of the space we had created together, listening to the sound of the ocean with candlelight. The conversations had deepened over the days, peeling back layers we had long held in place. This was no longer small talk—these were truths, raw and unfiltered, spoken aloud in a space where we felt safe enough to be seen.

And then, something happened.

During the initiation of Mama Ocello in the Nusta ceremony, I experienced a vision—one that I hadn't sought but one that had arrived nonetheless.

It was Mama Ocello, the divine mother energy of the Andean traditions. But she was more than just a presence—she was a guide, showing me something profound, something I wasn't expecting.

As I meditated, my breath was steady, my body was open to whatever came, and the vision unfolded before me. I saw each woman in our circle—not as they were now, but as their inner child.

Some clung tightly to their adult selves, their tiny hands gripping onto the women they had become, afraid to let go. Some stood back, hidden, hesitant, watching from the shadows. Others were open and free, playful and trusting, unburdened by the weight of the years.

It was breathtaking. There is so much truth, so much vulnerability.

And so, I spoke when we gathered later in our sharing circle.

I described what I had seen, allowing the words to flow from the same intuitive space, opening wider and broader within me.

At first, it felt like a gift.

Two women were visibly moved — eyes shining, hands pressed to their hearts, as though something unspoken had finally been acknowledged. Their inner children had been seen. They had been recognized in a way that perhaps they hadn't been in years, maybe even decades.

But then, something shifted.

Two others reacted differently.

Their bodies tensed, and their eyes darkened. The energy around the table grew heavier, charged with something unspoken. One looked down, her jaw set, arms crossed tightly over her chest. The other exhaled sharply, almost as if she were shaking off an unwanted thought.

And suddenly, my certainty wavered.

Had I said too much? Had I overstepped? Was it not my place to share what I had seen?

The old, familiar panic rushed in, a reflex so ingrained in me that I didn't even realize I had already started shrinking, folding in on myself. What have I done wrong?

I barely heard the rest of the conversation. I sat there, nodding in the right places and smiling when necessary, but inside, I was retreating — pulling myself back into the safe, familiar role of making sure everyone else was comfortable, even at the expense of myself.

As I lay awake that night, the echoes of Maria Sakapana and Mama Ocello swirled within me.

Hadn't this been the very thing I was meant to release? Hadn't I stood beneath the sky, hands open, voice firm, and declared that I would no longer make myself small?

And yet, here I was — doing it again.

I tried to shake it off as I moved through the retreat space the following day. Maybe I had imagined the energy shift, overanalyzed, or made it all bigger in my mind than it was, but Cindy had seen. Of course, she had.

She caught me later in that effortless way she always did — never forceful, never confrontational, just quietly present.

We stood near the edge of the retreat grounds, the ocean stretching wide in front of us, the waves moving with their steady rhythm. She didn't start with small talk. She didn't soften the question. She looked at me, steady and knowing, and asked: "Why did you shrink?" I opened my mouth, ready with the usual excuses — *Oh, it was nothing. I was probably overthinking. I didn't want to make anyone uncomfortable* — but the words caught in my throat.

Because I knew she wouldn't let me lie to myself. I sighed, glancing down at the earth beneath my feet. Why had I shrunk? The answer was that I had seen something beautiful. Because I had spoken from a place of truth, when it wasn't received as expected, I immediately questioned myself instead of standing firm in what I knew to be accurate. Cindy nodded, her gaze soft but unwavering.

"You do that a lot," she said, and I felt the sting of recognition, a truth so sharp it left no room for denial. "You see things," she continued, "and you feel them deeply, but the moment someone else doesn't meet you there, you assume you're wrong. You shrink instead of realizing that maybe they just aren't ready."

She was right.

How many times had I dimmed myself for the comfort of others? How many times had I second-guessed my gifts, my wisdom, simply because someone else wasn't in a place to receive them?

The realization settled in my chest, heavy and undeniable.

This wasn't about them; it was about me, my voice, my truth, my knowing, and for the second time in just a few days, I made a choice: I would try not to shrink again. However, the truth is, this isn't a lesson you learn once and carry with ease forever. This is a pattern I still have to deal with today. It's so deeply ingrained that I have to actively choose, over and over again, to take up space, to use my voice, to stand in my truth.

Sometimes, I catch myself in the moment and correct course. I breathe, I hold firm, I remind myself that my voice is valid, and sometimes, the pattern gets the better of me. I shrink, I retreat, I let the old fears take hold, and before I even realize it, I'm making myself small again.

The difference? Now I see it. I recognize when I'm doing it. And each time, the choice to stand taller, to stay open, becomes a little easier. The truth is, the journey isn't about never shrinking again; it's about choosing not to — again and again — until one day, shrinking is no longer my instinct at all.

Despite all the deep healing, soul-searching, and profound moments of transformation, there was another side to this retreat — the bubble.

That sacred, untouchable space where the real world dissolves, time feels different, and where you somehow find yourself in moments of pure, unfiltered joy that stay with you forever.

And I have never laughed so much in my entire life as I did on this trip.

One particular moment stands out — a snorkelling trip that should have been a picture-perfect, leisurely day of sunshine, turquoise waters, and gentle ocean breezes. Of course, the universe had other plans.

It started with six women, bags in tow, hats, sunglasses, and sunscreen at the ready, standing expectantly on the shore, waiting to step gracefully onto our boat and glide across the ocean like something out of a travel magazine. We should have known.

We should have known when the man organizing the trip handed us one single waterproof bag to share with all of us. One, but we were still optimistic — until we saw the boat. Or rather, the ship that refused to be launched.

We watched as the men in charge of launching it struggled, heaved, and pushed, their energy escalating with every failed attempt. The sea was rough, but this wasn't meant to be such an ordeal. Minutes passed, then twenty, and as more men descended onto the boat like warriors preparing for battle, something became hilariously obvious — we were witnessing masculine energy in its purest, most determined form.

The strategy. The competition. The sheer force of will. They weren't working with the sea. They were fighting it, and finally — after one last heroic effort, a collective grunt, and what I can only assume was a test of pride rather than practicality — the boat surrendered and slid into the sea like a great conquered beast.

We erupted into uncontrollable laughter because there was something so profoundly symbolic. How often had we seen this energy play out in our lives? The push, the force, the sheer determination to overpower something rather than just working with it? It was the perfect, unplanned lesson in contrast.

Here we were, six women standing in our soft, open, feminine energy, watching as the men around us fought the sea instead of moving with it, but, of course, we weren't thinking about any of that at the time. At the time, we were crying with laughter, clambering onto the boat, blissfully unaware that the universe wasn't done with us yet.

If we had thought, even for a second, that this would be a peaceful, luxurious boat ride, we were very wrong. The moment we set off, the wind picked up. What had started as a gentle ocean breeze quickly turned into something out of a comedy sketch.

You know those stage plays where someone stands on the side and throws buckets of water at the actors? That was us. Except it wasn't buckets. It was the ocean. Wave after wave crashed over us, blinding us, soaking us, flooding the boat to the point where you couldn't tell if you were laughing or just gasping for air. Then there were the waves — the kind that lifted you out of your seat just long enough to make you question your life choices.

I would have held onto my hat, but I was holding onto my soul at this point. Somehow, we made it to the atoll, although the universe wasn't done playing with us.

Typically, atolls are like paradise-like slices — calm and peaceful, where you gently step off your boat and wade through crystal-clear waters.

Not today. The tide was in, the wind was high, and the waves were fierce, and this, right here, is where feminine energy took centre stage because while the other boats around us emptied as people leaped eagerly into the water, our boat?

We sat right where we were.

Six women, arms crossed, watching the chaos unfold—and without a single spoken word, deciding: Nope. Not today. Well—most of us weren't.

One of our group members was braver (or more reckless) than the rest and made it into the water. Then, he disappeared. Not in a dramatic way. She just… wasn't there.

Suddenly, we spotted her, not in the water, but on another boat.

We later found out that the boat had nudged her—and a group of strangers had pulled her up onto their deck like some unexpected rescue mission, and at the time, we had no idea what had happened. We just sat there, soaking wet, watching one of our own suddenly appear on another boat entirely and lose it.

We laughed so hard we couldn't breathe because at this point? What else could we do? The universe had taken over well and truly.

By the time we left the atoll, we had stopped fighting it. We knew what was coming. We embraced it. The waves, the wind, and the water were no longer an attack. It was just part of the ride; maybe that was the real lesson. Sometimes, life is just chaos, comedy, crashing waves, and belly-aching laughter. Sometimes, the universe doesn't send you a quiet, profound moment of realization—it sends you a snorkelling trip gone wrong, a boat that won't move, and an ocean that decides you need a good dunking. You can't fight it. You must surrender, laugh, and let the waves take you exactly where you're meant to go.

There are moments in life when laughter takes over—not the polite, contained kind, but the kind that erupts from somewhere deep inside you, shaking loose things you didn't even know you were holding onto. The kind that steals your breath and leaves you doubled over, helpless, tears streaming down your face. The kind where you lock eyes with someone and completely lose it all over again, even when you've just managed to catch your breath.

This trip gave me that kind of laughter—not once, not twice, but over and over again—laughter that broke through years of holding it all together. I didn't realize I was still carrying laughter that shattered walls. The laughter felt like a remembering—of joy, freedom, and who I was before life made me careful.

On this trip, I laughed like I hadn't laughed in years—wild, abandoned, utterly unfiltered joy.

It wasn't just the absurdity of what was happening—the ridiculous boat ride, the universe throwing chaos at us like it had a personal vendetta. It was the shared experience, the deep connection, the sheer permission to let go because when you laugh like that—really laugh—you aren't performing. You aren't thinking about how you look or what comes next. You are entirely, beautifully present, and that? That is freedom.

The Goddess had awakened within me—not in some distant, mythical sense, but in a visceral, undeniable, and deeply real way. She had risen in the quiet moments of truth, in the rawness of initiation, in the power of my voice reclaiming itself. She had moved through the sacred stillness of healing, through the wild, unfiltered joy of laughter, through the surrender to life's chaos and beauty alike. However, the real test was not here, in this safe, sacred bubble — it was out there, in the world I had temporarily stepped away from. Could I carry her with me? Could I hold onto this power, this knowing, this unshakable sense of self when the emails flooded in, when the meetings started, when the weight of responsibility settled back onto my shoulders?

I didn't know the answer yet, but what I did know was this: I was not the same woman who had arrived at this retreat. As I packed my bags and prepared to return, I whispered a silent promise to myself — I would not forget.

CHAPTER 9:
From Rituals to Reality

The moment I stepped back into my house, I felt the emptiness.

Not of the space itself—my home was beautiful, carefully curated, a reflection of everything I had worked for. But the silence? That was deafening.

Just days ago, I had been surrounded by women, by laughter, by the rhythm of the ocean, by the sacred rituals that had cracked me open and stitched me back together in ways I didn't even know I needed. Now, it was just me. The walls stood still, the air undisturbed, and the reality of everyday life came crashing in with the force of grief, and I couldn't stop crying. Not just because I missed the retreat—though I did, achingly so—but because it felt as if I had stepped into an entirely different world where everything was the same except me.

The emails, the responsibilities, the mundane routines—it all felt so jarring and distant from the world I had just left. It was as if the retreat had happened in another lifetime, and yet the imprint of it was still alive within me, raw and exposed.

Then there was the music.

Cindy had created a playlist—a beautiful, haunting collection of songs that had soundtracked our journey. Each song was tied to a memory, a moment, a feeling so deep it had become woven into the fabric of my experience. I pressed play, letting the first few notes fill the room, and suddenly, I was back there. Music has a way of doing that. It transports you, pulls you through time, and makes you feel things you thought you had safely tucked away. The lyrics—the same ones I had heard—now carried a different weight and meaning. It was as if my experience had rewritten them, each word resonating with a depth I had never noticed before.

When you change, the world around you doesn't stay the same. Even the songs sound different; months later—even now—whenever I listen to that playlist, I hear something new. New lessons, new truths, new layers I hadn't uncovered before. The songs continued to evolve, just as I did, and then, just like that, it was time to go back to work.

The emails were waiting. The meetings were booked. The firm structure of everyday life wrapped itself around me again, and with it came the well-meaning but impossible question: "How was your holiday?" I would pause, searching for the words—but where did I begin?

How do you explain to someone that you didn't just go on a holiday; you stepped into something sacred? How do you describe how the ocean and the wind felt like whispers from something greater than yourself? How do you explain the power of a circle of women, of voices rising in unison, of rituals so profound they changed you on a cellular level? How do you put into words the way you broke open and stitched yourself back together and found pieces of yourself you didn't even realize were missing?

I tried. I'd start with something small, something light. "It was amazing. So beautiful. Life-changing." They would nod, waiting for more, expecting stories of cocktails by the pool, lazy afternoons in the sun, sightseeing, and relaxation.

How could I tell them that, instead, I had stood in the ceremony, hands pressed to the earth, tears streaming down my face as I let go of things I had been carrying for years? That I had found myself sobbing in the wind, speaking truths I had been too afraid to say out loud? That I had awakened something ancient, fierce, and powerful within me. So I would smile and say, "Yeah, it was incredible, "because some things can't be explained. Some things can only be felt, and the most challenging part is returning and realizing that not everyone can feel it with you.

Except for the women who were there. They understand. They always will.

At first, I thought the most challenging part of returning was the disconnection—feeling like I had changed while everything else had stayed the same. But I soon realized something even more confronting: how people reflected things on me.

I had spent days in a space of love, openness, and deep healing, surrounded by women who held space without judgment. But here? Back in the real world? The energy was different. People triggered me.

A comment in a meeting that felt dismissive.

A colleague whose energy clashed with mine.

A situation that pulled me into old patterns of people-pleasing, proving, or retreating.

I immediately felt familiar tension rising, and I instinctively shrank, reacted, and took things personally.

And then I remembered something I had learned on retreat.

People Are Mirrors

Some mirrors reflect love, warmth, and support, reminding us of the beauty within us. But others? They reflect the things we don't want to see.

The lessons we still need to learn. The wounds we haven't yet healed. The patterns we thought we had outgrown but find ourselves repeating.

One of the hardest mirrors for me is people in positions of power. They speak with authority, take up space without hesitation, and expect to be listened to, not questioned.

They trigger something deep inside me—the part of me that still shrinks, that still feels small, that still hesitates to use my voice because the truth is, I have spent years giving my power away. Not in obvious ways, but in the tiny, almost imperceptible moments—the times I didn't challenge something I disagreed with, the times I softened my words so I wouldn't seem "too much," the times I let someone else's confidence override my knowing.

So when I sit across from someone who effortlessly owns their authority, I don't just see them—I see all the moments I didn't, and that is the real challenge of mirrors. It's not just about what someone else is doing. It's about what it awakens in you.

Then, there's the mirror of emotion. I have always been deeply empathetic—I feel everything, speak with emotion, and lead with care, and yet, the world is full of people who don't. People who are detached, logical, cut-and-dry, and who move through conversations without warmth and connection; truthfully, I struggle with them because I don't understand how someone can hear pain and not acknowledge it or respond with facts when a situation calls for feeling. How can they make decisions without considering the human impact? I used to think this was just a personality clash. But in truth, it's another mirror because maybe their emotional distance isn't just a reflection of who they are.

Maybe it's a challenge to who I am.

Maybe their presence is here to teach me that not everyone will understand me in my depth, and that's okay. My empathy is my strength, but it is not everyone's language.

I cannot expect people to feel like I do—but I can still stand in my truth, even when they don't understand it.

The hardest thing about mirrors is that they don't lie. They show us exactly where we still have work to do. They reveal where we still shrink, react, and expect others to change instead of owning our transformation. Maybe the real lesson isn't to fight the reflections but to learn from them.

I recognized that every person who triggers something in me is offering me a choice: to react from my wounds or to rise from my wisdom, and so I tried. Oh, how I really tried, but trying to hold onto my balance—to keep learning, to stay open, to not fall back into old patterns—became hard.

It was one thing to feel strong in the sacred space of the retreat, surrounded by women who reflected love, truth, and deep connection. In the real world, where do people expect me to be the same as I was before? That was the actual test.

Yet one truth became more apparent than ever:

To be happy, I had to be fully, unapologetically myself. I had to speak my truth, even when it felt uncomfortable. I had to own my voice, even when it shook. Most importantly, I had to learn to love myself. Being single was something I had long been used to. It wasn't new.

I had done the dating sites, the endless cycle of sifting through messages, reading profiles, and trying to find something real among the noise. The texts that led nowhere. The connections that fizzled. The exhausting feeling of searching for something I couldn't quite name, and after the retreat, I just stopped.

I didn't want it anymore. Not like that, because, for the first time, I truly understood what I had learned at the Goddess retreat. Love starts with you. Not in a cliché way, not in a "self-love fixes everything" way, but in a way that felt bone-deep and unshakable.

I wasn't looking for someone to complete me. I wasn't waiting for someone to validate me.

I wasn't searching for love outside of myself anymore because I had finally started to find it within.

For the first time, I wasn't looking for someone to complete me.

I wasn't searching for love outside of myself.

Because I had finally started to find it within.

And yet, something still felt incomplete.

Self-love is not a final destination. It's a practice, a choice, a constant unfolding. And as much as I had grown, as much as I had learned to stand in my truth, the real world kept testing me.

The noise, the expectations, the push and pull of everything I had once been. I was holding onto my balance, but just barely, and that's when I felt it—the call. It was not just a desire but a deep knowing. I needed to go further, to sit in more profound stillness, to listen in a new way, to surrender fully to whatever came next. I followed the pull without fully knowing why.

To a place where the earth itself spoke. Where medicine wasn't just something you took—but something you became. Where healing didn't come from fixing—but from remembering.

I didn't know it yet, but I was about to step into another kind of awakening.

The second time, I knew it was something more.

After the Goddess retreat, Cindy had never really left my life. She was always there—on the end of the phone, in Zoom meetings, listening, reflecting, gently pointing out the mirrors I still needed to face. She wasn't just a guide in the sacred spaces of retreat—she was a presence, a quiet but unwavering force that kept me accountable for my growth.

So when she spoke to me about another retreat—a Sacred Medicine journey in Mukuru—I knew I couldn't ignore it. It wasn't just an invitation. It was a pull—a knowing. I felt in my gut that this was where I was going. Healing isn't linear. It's not a moment of realization, neatly wrapped with a bow. It's a path, a process, a series of breadcrumbs leading you deeper and deeper into yourself.

And so, I followed them to the land, medicine, and a more profound awakening. I had no idea what I was about to step into, but something inside me whispered:

Go.

CHAPTER 10:

Sacred Medicine - A Deeper Awakening

The land stretched before us, vast and untouched, as if it had been waiting for our arrival. The air was thick with something I couldn't quite name—a presence, an energy, an ancient knowing. This was not just a place; it was something alive.

We stepped out onto the earth, the dust rising gently around our feet. In the distance, I heard them before I saw them—the deep, rhythmic chanting of the Maasai warriors. Their voices rose and fell like a heartbeat, syncing with the land.

They approached us in formation, their bodies strong, their presence unshakable. This was no ordinary welcome—this was a blessing.

One by one, they tapped the earth with their shields, a ritualistic cleansing, calling on the spirits of the land to prepare for our arrival. The sound was steady and grounding, as if they were waking something deep within the soil and us.

We were not just guests. We were being received as queens.

I stood between Cindy and my friend—the three of us, once again, stepping into something unknown together. The Maasai warriors surrounded us, their voices weaving into the air, their chants merging with the wind. At that moment, the weight of the journey and my transformation settled over me. I felt seen, honoured, humbled, and, more than anything in this wilderness, at home.

Then, as if on cue, one of the warriors stepped forward, his face unreadable, his voice deep with amusement. "We have made a drink for you," he said, gesturing to a large vessel. "Sheep's blood."

I felt Cindy shift beside me, my friend's eyes widening. My stomach turned slightly, and for a moment, I wondered if this was some initiation—a test of strength, a test of spirit. Then, as they lifted the jug to pour, we saw the liquid—not blood but normal fresh juice.

Their faces broke into broad smiles, deep laughter rolling through the air.

It was a joke—their humour, warmth, and way of welcoming us not just with reverence but with playfulness, which I was later to learn who their true nature is.

I exhaled, a slow smile spreading as I took the cup. The first sip was rich, slightly tart, and cool against the afternoon's heat.

They sang as we drank, their voices blending into something almost otherworldly—a sound that instantly rooted me to the earth and lifted me into the sky.

And in that moment, something shifted.

I had come here for healing. I had come here for answers. I had come here searching for something I couldn't quite name.

But this?

This was more than a retreat. This was a remembering of the land, the sacredness that lives in all things, and myself.

In Mukuru, the land feels alive. Surrounded by mountains and held by the vast open sky, this place was unlike anywhere I had ever been. It carried an energy that was both ancient and immediate, as if every rock, every breeze, every shifting shadow held the whispers of something sacred. And then, there she was — Kilimanjaro.

She stood in the distance, her presence commanding yet serene. The Maasai spoke of her as if she were alive, watching over them, shifting her appearance throughout the day. Sometimes bare, sometimes draped in mist — her blanket, they called it. There was a deep reverence in their voices, a knowing that this land was more than earth and stone; it was spirit, memory, and history woven together. However, I felt that Mount Mukuru held the greatest power here.

The only sacred mountain of the Maasai in Mukuruland is a place once utterly inaccessible to outsiders. For over 200 years, this land had been known only to them — protected, untouched. But now, for reasons they alone understood, they had chosen to open it, to share its holiness with a select few, not for money or tourism but for something far more meaningful — a way to feed the children of Mukuru and support the schools that carried their future.

I was standing in a place few had ever been invited to, and I could feel that truth in my bones.

My home for this journey was a cave carved into the land by the Maasai themselves. There were no doors, only open space, an unbroken view of Kilimanjaro in all her changing beauty. The cave was modern yet deeply rooted in tradition—adorned with Maasai beadwork, handcrafted furniture, and woven crafts that spoke of patience, skill, and a culture that creates with intention.

A small table and chairs sat outside, perfectly placed to take in the vastness of the land. Here, time didn't move in hours and minutes but in the rhythm of nature, the shifting light, the steady heartbeat of the earth beneath me.

There was no separation between myself and the land. No walls, no locks, no barriers—only open sky, open earth, and open spirit.

A home where you could 'be'.

Every moment in Mukuru, I felt myself settling more deeply into the rhythm of the land. There was no rush, no urgency—only the steady pulse of nature, the quiet wisdom that seemed to hum beneath my feet. The boundaries between myself and the earth felt thinner here as if I were being absorbed into something ancient, something greater than myself.

The Maasai moved with this same quiet knowing. Their presence was both grounding and expansive, reminding me that sacredness isn't just in rituals—it's in how you walk, listen, and honour what cannot be seen.

Each day in Mukuru felt like a lesson, a quiet unfolding of something I had always known but somehow forgotten. The land was teaching me—not through words but through experience. One of the most profound lessons came through the elements.

The Maasai believe that earth, water, air, fire, and ether are not just forces of nature but sacred energies that live within us. Each one carries its wisdom, medicine, and reflection of who we are, and so, over the days that followed, we honoured each one.

Cindy had organised a ceremony in a special cave, different from the one I called home. It was a place far older and far more sacred, a place where their elders had gathered, where voices from the past still lingered in the stone, and where the unseen world felt just as present as the one in front of me.

It was here that we would drink cacao—not just as a warm, earthy liquid in our hands but as a doorway to spirit, to the earth, to ourselves. I didn't know then just how much this ceremony would shift something inside me, but I would soon find out.

The journey to the cave was silent and reverent.

We walked through the land, each step pulling us deeper into something unseen, something ancient. This was not the cave where I slept, not the space I had come to know as home. This was different. This was sacred.

The Maasai led us toward a place touched by centuries of ceremony—a cave where their ancestors had gathered, their elders had prayed, and the spirit of the land still lingered. As we approached, the air shifted. It was subtle but undeniable—a weight, a presence, a knowing.

The cave loomed before us, its entrance dark and open, as if inviting us in. This was not a place to take lightly. The Maasai understood this, so before we entered, they did what they had always done—cleaning the space. Their voices rose in song, a chant that did not just fill the cave but became part of it. The sound wrapped around the stone walls, vibrating through the ground beneath us, moving through the air like an invisible current.

They tapped the earth with their staffs — steady, deliberate — calling the space to attention, waking something within it.

Then, as quickly as the sound had come, it was gone. There was silence — a silence so deep that it felt alive.

We stepped inside the air cooler, the space heavy with the presence of something unseen but deeply felt. We sat in a circle, the warmth of the cacao in our hands, the scent rich and grounding. This was a drink meant to open the heart and bring us closer to the spirit of the earth.

I lifted the cup to my lips, the liquid bitter yet smooth, its warmth spreading through me. Something inside me softened.

And then, as I sat in stillness, something else happened.

The Maasai, who had filled the space with their voices moments ago, had become completely silent. They stood above us, their staffs raised in ceremony, their presence unwavering.

They did not speak, or move. They simply held space. I didn't know it at the time. I didn't see the quiet strength in their stance or the unspoken prayers they carried. I only knew that I felt held.

Held by the earth. Held by the space and held by something greater than myself. I knew then that I was meant to be grounded. I am meant to stand firm in who I am.

It was only later that I learned what had happened — that as we drank, as we connected with the cacao, the Maasai had stood in silent reverence, their staffs lifted, and their energy wrapped around us like an invisible embrace.

Even in stillness, they guided us, holding three women in a safe ceremonial space with strength and softness I had never felt before. In that cave, I felt the lesson of the earth settle inside me.

The ceremony ended, but its impact lingered. We stepped out of the cave and back into the open air, and I felt the warmth of the land welcoming us once again. The sky stretched wide, its vastness mirroring the stillness I felt within. There was something profound in that silence — a transition, a moment between worlds, between what was and what was yet to come.

And then, it was time to honour water the next day.

For our Water Ceremony, we walked to a place where a river once ran, its path now a stretch of cracked earth. I had expected water to mean flow, movement, and softness — but there was only an absence. Yet, the Maasai didn't see it as empty. They saw it as a promise.

"The river always returns," one of them said. "Just because you do not see it now does not mean it is gone."

The words hit me harder than I expected. How many times had I believed I had lost something forever? How often had I grieved parts of myself, thinking they would never return? My softness. My joy. My voice. What if they were like the river? What if they Weren't gone — just waiting for the right season to return?

I knelt, running my fingers through the dry earth. Closing my eyes, I listened — not for water, but for the wisdom in its absence. And in that stillness, I understood. The river was never truly gone. It was only waiting.

It felt like a lesson in trust—to believe that what is meant for us will always find its way back. At that moment, clarity settled within me—I was never empty, I was never broken, and I was waiting for the rains to return.

As the sun slowly descended, casting golden hues across the land, we climbed Life Mountain. The sky shifted from gold to amber to deep indigo, marking the transition from day to night. The Maasai could have easily sprinted up that mountain without breaking a sweat. This land was part of them, woven into their very being. But they didn't. Instead, they moved with us, for us.

They matched our pace, ensuring no stone was too uneven, no step too treacherous, no thorny bush waiting to catch us unaware. Every movement was intentional, protective, and steady. They weren't just leading us up the mountain; they were holding space for us, ensuring we made the journey safely. They were the perfect harmony of strength and gentleness. Power, not in dominance but in presence. It was the purest expression of the divine masculine I had ever witnessed.

We could all learn from this, and I couldn't help but compare it to leadership. Authentic leadership isn't about charging ahead and expecting others to keep up. It's about guiding, holding, and protecting without taking away the experience of the journey itself—something that, at times, I know I've forgotten.

What followed was an evening to remember. We visited the Whispering Cave, a space deeply connected to the earth—a truly sacred place. The Maasai took great care in entering, and as we removed our shoes and socks, walking barefoot on the planet into the hollow, we could feel the reverence. Once again, they held space for us.

Leaning into the hollows, we felt the air rising through the land—a combination of stillness and movement, as though voices were speaking softly in the wind, soothing and nurturing.

As the Maasai lit the sacred fire, we made our way a few hundred yards away to carry out our thanks and ceremony before returning to find them quietly huddled by the flames. And so, we made the slow journey back down the mountain with no fear of the darkness or the wilderness—just a deep knowing and trust in the safety of the circle that held us.

I have something to share that brings me great joy today. One of our evenings, sitting by the fire with the Maasai, was filled with incredible joy and laughter. Phillipo and our guide told us that the Maasai were giggling about a story one of the elders had shared in the village—about how he had hugged a woman today for the first time in his life.

Unbeknownst to us, the Maasai do not traditionally hug. And believe me when I say that all three of us were huggers from the moment we arrived. Without ever meaning to offend, it was simply second nature— we hugged them when they took care of us, when we shared a moment, or at the end of the day. Little did we know that this had caused great amusement and joy among the Maasai.

And so, just as the land and its people had left their imprint on us, we had unknowingly left our imprint on them.

On our final day, we were guided to the Wisdom Tree. It stood tall and unwavering, its gnarled roots gripping the earth as if anchoring the past to the present. This tree had witnessed generations of stories, had seen warriors grow into elders, and had held the prayers of those who came before us. It symbolized endurance, knowing, and the silent wisdom that comes with time.

We each took a moment beneath its vast branches, placing our hands on its bark, feeling the ancient pulse of the land move through us. The Maasai spoke of this tree as a keeper of knowledge, a bridge between the physical and the spiritual. Beneath its shade, they told us that wisdom is not something to be chased but received in stillness. To listen, be open, and allow the truth to reveal itself.

I closed my eyes, allowing my journey to settle within me. Everything I had experienced—the teachings of the elements, the quiet guidance of the Maasai, the way the land had embraced me—led to this moment. The Wisdom Tree was not just a destination but a reflection of what had always been within me.

As the wind rustled through its leaves, I felt a deep peace. I understood that wisdom is not found in the frantic search for answers but in surrendering to knowing they will come in their own time. As I stood beneath the arms of the ancient tree, I knew I was leaving Mukuru with more than I had come for. I was going with a part of the land, and it, with a part of me.

But the journey was not over.

The lessons I had gathered, the whispers of the land, and the strength I had found within myself were leading me to something more profound. The next step was not about searching but about stepping fully into who I was meant to be—to trust my voice, to own my presence, to embody the goddess within me.

And so, as I turned away from the Wisdom Tree and back toward the path ahead, I knew that my journey was shifting.

The next chapter is about what I had learned and how I would live it.

CHAPTER 11:
The Goddess and her Shadows

For so long, I searched for the light. I reached for healing, growth, and the bright and shining version of myself — the one who had overcome, who had risen, and who stood fully in her power. I believed that to be whole, I had to seek the light and turn away from the dark.

I was wrong.

This has been my greatest lesson, my most profound experience, and the teaching that continues to shape me.

I thought I understood that true self-love is not found in chasing the light but in embracing the shadow. In reality, I had only scratched the surface.

My first real encounter with my shadows came after returning from my medicine retreat. I had experienced a nightmare — one that felt disturbingly real as if it had spilled into my waking life. Heavy and unsettling, the emotions lingered long after I woke up, blurring the line between dream and reality.

When I shared this with Cindy, shadows first came into the light for me — or at least, the first layer of my understanding. She spoke to me about the parts of ourselves we suppress, the wounds we refuse to look at, and how they never truly disappear. Instead, they live in the background, subtly influencing our emotions, behaviours, and choices.

Encouraged to explore my shadows, I began journaling about everything I had done or experienced that carried shame or guilt. I will not lie — it was uncomfortable. I had to dig deep and sit with moments I had long hidden. There were parts of me I had successfully buried, memories I had locked away, wounds I had convinced myself no longer existed. However, I was committed.

I did this work for weeks, believing I was embodying my shadows. I told myself I was facing them, integrating them, making peace with them.

Yet, I have learned that we are only ever asked to face what we are ready for. At that time, those were the shadows I was capable of confronting, and yet life has a way of presenting us with the deeper layers when we least expect them.

Then came an event that shook my world.

The shadows descended upon me — I could feel them swirling, trying to claim me. Everything I thought I had learned suddenly seemed to slip through my fingers.

Circumstances brought a natural ending to that phase of my work. At the time, it felt like a loss — but in hindsight, it was a sacred redirection

A job I had woven my soul into. A role I cared deeply about — a place where I worked alongside a family of colleagues I treasured. Everything I believed I stood for — a successful businesswoman, respected, safe —

was suddenly pulled from under me. It could have sent me spinning.

And, in many ways, it did.

I truly felt as though I had been thrown into a vast, dark ocean—tossed around by waves far bigger than me, struggling desperately to keep afloat. I kicked, grasped, and thrashed, trying to keep my head above water. The more I struggled, the more the sea seemed to claim me. The fear took hold, dragging me deeper.

I had a choice.

Did I keep fighting against the current, exhausting myself in the process? Or did I surrender—*truly surrender*—to the dark ocean, allowing myself to breathe deeply, let go, and trust?

The moment I stopped fighting, something shifted.

I stopped thrashing and allowed myself to float. My body softened, and my breath steadied. I was no longer drowning; I was being carried. And that was when I started to bob along the waves rather than be consumed by them.

This was the truth I had been resisting. Shadowwork is not about *fighting the darkness*. It is about *surrendering* to it, trusting that even in the depths, you are safe.

I told myself this was a gift—a gift of time—to spend with my grandsons, to travel, and to reassess what career would bring me joy.

In truth, I was burying my emotions. I had convinced myself this was an opportunity—a chance to follow my dreams and aspirations. I refused to wallow in self-pity or anger. Instead, I decided I would pick myself up and embrace the change. My intentions were good: *I would not sink into the shadows. I have so much to live for and so much love around me. All will be well.*

But this was not shadow work.

This was denial.

Over the next few weeks, I drifted between enjoying the freedom of not working and battling days when I became my worst enemy. I grew judgemental of myself.

Why am I feeling this way?

Why can't I get motivated today?

I have so much to be grateful for, so why can't I pick myself up and get on with it?

The frustration with myself built up, layer by layer. I was not just feeling low; I was punishing myself for feeling low. I was not just struggling; I was criticising myself for struggling. And the more I judged myself, the deeper I sank.

Have you ever stopped to listen to the language you use on yourself? Not just the obvious thoughts, but the whispers, the passing comments, the casual self-criticisms that slip out so effortlessly?

Once you start paying attention, you hear it everywhere.

"I am not any good at that."

"I am not brave enough to try that."

"Sorry about how I look today; I wasn't feeling myself."

"I should just pull myself together."

We say these things without thinking, brushing them off as nothing.

Yet they are not nothing.

Words have weight. They shape our reality. They become the voice we wake up to and fall asleep with — the voice that either nurtures or destroys us.

Despite this, many of us move through life without questioning it. We would never speak to a friend the way we talk to ourselves, yet we carry on, daily, reinforcing beliefs that tell us we are less than or not enough.

I had not realized how much my self-talk was feeding my shadows. Yet once I heard it — once I *genuinely* heard it — I could not ignore it anymore.

There was a person at work whom I did not get along with. We were opposites, and honestly, I found it incredibly difficult to work with them.
Yet, looking back, they were my most significant teacher — my mirror.

Carl Jung, the father of shadow work, spoke about projection — the unconscious way we disown parts of ourselves by seeing them in others. When we judge, criticize, or react strongly to someone, it is often because they are reflecting on something hidden within us. This is the mirror effect.

So I took a long, deep look.

I did not like what I found, and that was precisely the point.

In the mirror of this person, I saw all the things I hated and fought against. The uncomfortable truth was that I could be those things, too. I could be rigid, unsympathetic, harsh, and controlling — all the qualities I had always judged so harshly in others.

Yet, each of these traits held a gift.

My rigidity had given me stability and reliability — qualities that had been essential while raising two children on my own. My discipline had kept us safe. Even my harshness had served a purpose; it had given me clarity in difficult times and protected me when I needed strength.

To truly embrace shadow work means diving deep into everything that triggers you — the things you dislike, the hidden traits, and the parts of yourself you have spent years rejecting. It means bringing these aspects into the light and accepting them — wholly, completely, and without shame.

Healing does not come from overcoming. It comes from accepting.

It is about standing in front of the mirror and seeing all of myself — not just the parts that shine, but the parts that ache, that rage, that fear — and choosing not to turn away.

To be a genuine goddess and truly whole is to love all of it.

We have been conditioned to believe that healing means becoming something different, something better. However, true healing is not about changing who you are but embracing who you have always been.

Your shadows are not your weakness; they are your wisdom.

When you stop resisting your shadows and start loving them, you will understand what it truly means to be free.

And that is when the goddess within you awakens.

CHAPTER 12:

Integration - The True Work of Living the Goddess Within

There was a time when I believed awakening was the destination. Once I had gathered all the lessons, healed all the wounds, and stood in my power, I would finally arrive—whole, complete, untouchable.

But now I know the truth.

Awakening is not the end. It is the beginning.

The goddess within is not something we achieve. She is not waiting at the finish line, ready to crown us for our efforts. She has been here all along, waiting for us to remember.

I once thought that healing meant reaching a point where nothing could shake me, where I would no longer question myself or stumble. I thought that once I had "done the work," I would be untouchable, but life doesn't work that way.

There are still moments when I trip when old patterns whisper my name, and when doubt creeps in like a shadow at dawn. Only now do I meet them differently—not with resistance but with presence, not with fear but with trust. I have learned that living in my power does not mean never falling—it means knowing how to rise.

This journey has been about shedding, about unraveling the layers of conditioning that kept me small, and about unlearning the need to prove, to please, to be anything other than who I am at my core.

And now, as I step into this new chapter, I no longer strive to become.

I choose to be.

To be in my voice.

To be in my worth.

To be in my truth.

And in doing so, I permit others to do the same.

But what does this look like in *daily* life?

For me, it has meant redefining success—not as a measure of what I achieve, but as a reflection of how I feel. It has meant trusting that my worth is not tied to productivity, that I do not have to *earn* rest, and that softness is as powerful as strength. To follow joy in my life.

It has meant embracing stillness as much as action, learning to sit in quiet spaces without needing to fill them. It has meant honouring my emotions without labelling them as "good" or "bad"—understanding that sadness is not a failure, anger is not a weakness, and fear is not a sign of unworthiness.

This is the work. This is the embodiment.

Something I have come to know with certainty is that we often look outward for healing, change, and support—seeking answers from external sources and guidance in the world around us. But the true secret is this: *everything we seek already lies within.*

For years, I searched for the missing piece—the teacher, the book, the practice that would unlock my healing. I thought I would be complete if I could learn and find one more insight.

But healing is not about finding something that is missing. It is about remembering what has always been there.

We have been conditioned to believe that transformation comes from something outside of us—a mentor, a teacher, a sacred space, a new experience. In reality, these things only serve as mirrors, reflecting back what we already carry deep within our souls.

When we silence the noise, when we stop seeking validation, when we allow ourselves to be still, we begin to hear the quiet truth that has been whispering to us all along:

We are enough.

We have always been enough.

This is the essence of living the goddess within.

It is no longer about *searching* but about *reclaiming.*

For so long, I believed love was something to be found—something outside of me—a missing piece waiting to be discovered in another person. Like many of us, I grew up with the stories of love we are told:

The fairy tales, the great romances, and the belief that when we find the right person, everything will fall into place. I believe that love comes from someone else in its most accurate form.

But now I know the truth.

The love we seek—the deep, unbreakable, unwavering love—has always been within.

For years, I searched for love outside of myself, believing that if I were chosen, loved, and *enough* for someone else, then I would finally be whole. I measured my worth through relationships, acceptance, and external validation. And in doing so, I dimmed my light. I silenced my voice.

I became smaller in relationships, afraid of being *too much*.

I withheld my truth, afraid of scaring people away.

I shaped myself into what I thought others wanted rather than standing fully in who I was.

And the irony? The more I abandoned myself, the further I felt from love.

True love—the kind that does not waver, break, or leave—does not come from another person. It is the love we cultivate within ourselves. It is the love we give ourselves in the quietest moments, in the deepest of wounds, in the parts of us we once deemed unworthy.

We often talk about attracting the right person, about manifesting the love we desire. But real love does not come from *looking* for someone to complete us. It comes from becoming so full within ourselves that love is drawn to us.

Love is not about finding someone who fills the empty spaces inside us; it is about becoming whole on our own so that when love arrives, it is a reflection, not a rescue.

I spent years believing love was something to earn. What if I were pleasing, quiet, agreeable, and *lovable* enough? Then love would stay? But the love that must be *proven* is not love at all.

For years, I searched for love outside of myself, believing that when I found 'the one,' I would finally feel whole. Only love was never something I had to see—it was something I had to create. And so, I have started treating myself how I longed for someone else to treat me. I no longer waited for someone to bring me flowers—I filled my home with them. Instead, I stopped waiting for validation, and it became my most significant source of love. I whispered kind words to myself in the mirror. I held myself in the dark moments, and in doing so, I became the love I had always sought.

I have learned to hold myself dear, to talk to myself kindly, to be curious about how I'm feeling, and to truly listen to myself and my body. Every day, I say to myself, "It doesn't matter what you do, what you say, or how you feel. I love you, Tina, unconditionally, and I am always here for you."

Have I found true love with someone? In the traditional sense, no—I am still single. That does not mean love is missing from my life. If anything, it means I am still unfolding, growing, and saying yes to life in ways I never have before.

The most incredible love story I have ever known is the one I am trying to build with myself and continue daily.

I truly and deeply know that the more I embrace life and explore, the more I honour and love myself, the brighter my light will shine. As I stand tall in my complete authenticity, love will not be something to search for — it will simply recognize me. The right love will meet me there, not to complete me, but to reflect the wholeness I already carry within.

So, I do not wait. I do not search. I do not question.

I trust.

I trust that true, expansive, unwavering love will arrive in its own time and way.

Until then, I will keep choosing myself. Again and again.

Because I am the great love of my life.

The real question is not: *When will I find love?*

The question is: *How deeply am I willing to love myself?*

The moment we embrace our own worth, the moment we stop looking for love outside of ourselves, we become magnetic — not just to romantic love but to deep, authentic connections of all kinds.

We stop chasing.

We stop performing.

We stop settling.

We no longer need love to *fill* us.

We become love itself.

And the people who are meant for us — the souls who see us, honour us, and meet us where we are — will find us *there*.

It is about trusting that we already hold the answers, that our intuition is our most excellent guide, and that true power comes not from external achievements but from deep inner knowing.

So, how do we integrate this into daily life?

We do it by choosing presence over urgency.

By embracing stillness as much as action.

By allowing ourselves to be as much as we do.

To live as the goddess within is to no longer define worth by productivity but by presence.

It is to know that thriving does not come from striving but from allowing.

It is about stepping boldly into our voice, not waiting for permission to be heard.

It is about owning our space in this world — not shrinking or apologising, but standing in the fullness of who we are.

This does not mean the work is over. The journey does not end here. It never does.

But now, as I walk forward, I do so with an unshakable knowing.

I am my healer.

I am my guide.

I am and always have been, whole.

And so are you.

If you take one thing from this journey, let it be this:

You are not broken.

You are not incomplete.

There is nothing within you that needs to be erased or hidden away.

You are already whole.

We have been conditioned to believe that healing means becoming something different, something better. However, true healing is not about changing who you are but embracing who you have always been.

Your shadows are not your weakness; they are your wisdom.

Your fears, wounds, and darkness hold the very lessons that will set you free.

Finding love is not external. It is within

So, I invite you to sit with yourself, just as you are.

To stop running.

To stop trying to fix what was never broken in the first place.

Instead, lean in, hold your own hand, speak to the parts of yourself that you have abandoned, and listen to what they have to say.

And above all, meet them with love.

When you stop resisting your shadows and start loving them, you will understand what it truly means to be free.

And that is when the goddess within you awakens.

This book is not the end of my story. If anything, it is just the beginning of a new chapter — one I have not yet written but one I am excited to live. I do not have all the answers, which is its beauty. Life is still unfolding, teaching, and guiding me to more profound truths. And so, as I close this chapter, I do not do so with certainty but curiosity. With openness. With trust. There is more to come — for me, for you, for all of us walking this path of awakening, and perhaps, one day, I will write the next book. Until then, I invite you to step into your own story, trust your path, and remember that you are already whole.

ACKNOWLEDGEMENT

This book is dedicated to my beautiful, strong mother, Christine Thursfield.

Thank you for your love, support, and the gift of life. Your strength, resilience, and unwavering belief in me have shaped the woman I am today. You have been my anchor, encourager, and quiet source of grace through every season.

And to Cindy Lobo — soul sister, guide, and sacred mirror. Thank you for walking this path beside me, holding space when I needed it most, and always reflecting my light back to me when I couldn't see it myself. Your wisdom, intuition, and friendship have been a true blessing woven into the fabric of this journey.

To the many women who have held me, healed me, and reminded me of my own power — thank you. Your presence, teachings, and energy work have been lifelines, initiations, and awakenings that called me home to myself.

To the mentors and teachers who shared their gifts so generously, thank you for expanding my perspective and encouraging me to remember who I truly am beneath all the layers.

To my dear friends — thank you for your laughter, love, and your listening hearts. You've cheered me on, lifted me up, and reminded me that I never walk alone.

To the unseen — my guides, my ancestors, and the divine energies that whispered this book into being — I honour you. Your presence has been felt in every word, every pause, every unfolding moment.

And finally, to every soul who picks up this book, thank you. You are part of this story now, and I hope these pages meet you with the same love, grace, and truth that shaped them.

www.ingramcontent.com/pod-product-compliance
Lightning Source LLC
Chambersburg PA
CBHW051606010526
44119CB00056B/797